Wild
APPROACH
LEADERSHIP

◆———————————◆

Ideas On Leadership From A Wild Life

David Viker

VIKER LEADERSHIP
PUBLISHING

Wild
APPROACH
LEADERSHIP

Ideas On Leadership From a Wild Life

© 2022 by David Viker

Printed in the United States of America.

ISBN-13:
979-8-218-00894-9-Paperback
979-8-218-00895-6- Hardcover

Library of Congress Control Number: 2022909649

Viker Leadership Publishing
Canton, Georgia

Contact David Viker at david.vikerleadership@gmail.com (email); @davidaviker (Facebook); and (678) 772-2055 (cell).

Table of Contents

Introduction

We Need A New Approach

We live in wild times. A global pandemic swept across our Earth to start the new decade and changed life and work as we know it. A great awakening to racial disparity shined light in dark places. The largest, smartest, and most diverse and connected workforce in the history of the world is vastly different than just 20 years ago. Work from home reshaped what the office looks like. Though we are more respectful of our teammates, more curious about other cultures, more receptive to feedback, and appear more open to new adventures than any workforce in history—and we communicate at historic levels through social media—*we rarely just talk and almost never deeply connect.* We know more about television reality show characters than our neighbors and office mates. Social media can be too much, "look at me!" and not enough, "how are you?" New apps on our phone are more likely to group some of us than connect more of us. In school our tests have individual answers of A, B, C, or D; we are not taught how to collaborate with others to solve complex problems. We are well prepared individually for the hours-long college *SAT*, but ill-prepared as adults to *s-i-t* through a half hour meeting with healthy conflict. Our classroom environment through grade school experience, vocational/technical training, or college was long on the "who, what, where, and when" of facts—technical solutions to specific problems— but short on the "why and how" of adaptive leadership to a wild world in rapid change.

We need a new approach. Even the traditions-focused military recognizes it. General Stanley McChrystal said, "As the world becomes

1

more complex, the importance of leaders will only increase. Even quantum leaps in artificial intelligence are unlikely to provide the personal will, moral courage, and compassion that good leaders offer."

The rate of change in how we work and who we work with demands a wildly different approach to leadership. With many leadership books starting to sound the same, I wrote Wild Approach Leadership to be wildly different. It is built on my many mistakes and lessons learned through four unique and wild facets of my life: a rough childhood, parent of three children born in three different decades, coach of more than 40 youth sports teams, and leader of more than 800 employees in a wildlife and natural resource agency for a 10-state area. I also draw from experiences and wisdom of others. I cite timeless advice from figures around the world. To prepare for *Wild Approach Leadership*, I read 112 books and dozens of articles about leadership and leadership development. I quote from 74 of those works here, but in some instances with a disagreement or different angle than the author. Throughout the book when wild approach leadership is written, it means a new and better approach.

In the spirit of a wildly different approach to a leadership book, I use a less traditional approach for this book's structure. Instead of long chapters that lead to one central point, it is more loosely organized in a smaller-section format. This book's format may be different than you are accustomed to, but I intentionally structured it in more digestible bites—tailor-made for the way people rapidly inhale information in our tweet, blog post, and Netflix quick-consume culture. One section flows to the next by way of ellipse…and before those of you who are more organized than the rest of us get too nervous, know that there is indeed structure to this book. *Wild Approach Leadership* is framed in two parts: Build It and Apply It. We build it with the four C's (Connection, Character, Collaboration, and Communication…who we are), and we apply it with the four Ps (People, Priorities, Policy, and Planning…what we do). Each chapter has nine or ten sections, and each are relatable stories in digestible bites. Your reaction a moment ago may have been, "oh no, the book ends with boring policy and planning." Fear not. Know that those two chapters were so named because I just couldn't think of more clever chapter names that start with the letter "P" to describe how we make good decisions (policy) and how best to think ahead (planning). Terms such as team member, team, or organization represent your work colleagues, agency, organization, sports team, or family with equal leadership applicability.

I took the temperature of a black bear deep in a forest with a thermometer, caught an alligator with my bare hands at night in the swamp, used explosives to blow a beaver dam that flooded a road, and handcuffed a drunk driver on a wildlife refuge. Those experiences, though, all felt less treacherous than the average staff meeting, job interview, or performance review. Wildlife conservation icon Aldo Leopold wrote in *A Sand County Almanac*, "…Our encounters with wild nature can reveal, not only interesting and useful observations about natural history, but important truths about human nature…a deep understanding of our place in the long scheme of things not only makes the world a more interesting place, but can give us direction…"[8] Though the paperwork I received upon graduation from the University of Florida says something about natural resource conservation with a wildlife ecology emphasis, it is my studies of wildly interesting human beings since then that will help most you advance your leadership development most. I wrote this book over eight years, as I led and learned, and it was a labor of love on lunch breaks, long flights, and late nights. *Wild Approach Leadership* draws on 50 years of living and laughing—while learning to lead.

To help you move your leadership forward, I reflect on my many mistakes as well as the mishaps and successes of others. Though I changed most names, the stories are all true.

3

While there are timeless leadership principles to live by—and I highlighted many in the pages that follow—there are wildly different approaches to leadership, more appropriate and effective than what history teaches or popular culture suggests. We will break the so-called Golden Rule, and also bend or break many outdated axioms so you can break free of their hold on your leadership growth. We will expose, explore, and in some cases explode old sayings such as:

➔ *"Treat everyone the same."*...No, treat everyone fairly and use approaches unique to the person

➔ *"Sticks and stones may break my bones, but words will never heart me."*...No, words matter the most and cut the deepest

➔ *"He's a born leader."*...No, there's no such thing. Leaders are made.

➔ *"She tells it like it is."*...No, she shares things through her unique frame of reference

➔ *"Fix the weakest employees."*...No, give our best energies to our best performers

➔ *"If you don't have something nice to say, don't say anything at all."*...No, often the kindest thing we can do is share critical feedback

➔ *"A boss shouldn't show weaknesses."*...No, admitting weakness is a strength

➔ *"Familiarity breeds contempt."*...No, it doesn't. It builds relationships, trust, and loyalty

➔ *"A leopard doesn't change its spots."*...Well, that's true for a leopard, but most people have tremendous capacity for change

➔ *"I didn't have time."*...No, we all have the same amount of time. Make it our priority.

➔ *"If it ain't broke, don't fix it."*... That approach will rarely result in new breakthroughs

➔ *"The more things change, the more they stay the same."*...No, change or die.

The Cambridge dictionary says that the word *wild* can be a noun, adverb, or adjective.[1] Wild the noun means a natural state or uncultivated or uninhabited region. We will go there to explore many natural mistakes, some newly cultivated ideas, and venture into a largely uninhabited region of leadership. The slang form of wild as an adjective means excellent, special, or unusual. Wild Approach Leadership may give you special and unusual results. Let's start with advice from a man with a wild nickname and a wildly successful coaching career. Paul "Bear" Bryant said, "When you make a mistake, there are only three things you should ever do about it: Admit it, learn from it, and don't repeat it." I then add one more, and it is the foundation of this book: share your mistakes with others in a memorable way.

Part I:

The 4 C's

CHAPTER 1

Connection — Strong Bonds Required

"YOU MUST HAVE TWO MOUTHS!"

I will venture to guess that all of us have said at one time or another that "he or she talks too much." Here's a question the former chairmen of Lockheed Martin once asked: "When was the last time you heard someone criticized for listening too much?" A phrase I heard a lot growing up was: "God gave us two ears and one mouth for a reason." I think that means I should listen twice as much as I talk, but that is difficult to put into practice.

It was just after sunrise on a seven-hour road trip from our home in north Georgia to Walt Disney World in central Florida. I began to stir. My wife, Mary, beside me, was quiet. Everyone was. Our two teenaged children, Dane and Taylor, flanked the youngest, Matthew, asleep in his car seat. The long silence in the car was comfortable for others, but it agitated me. I describe myself as an energetic, uninhibited extrovert, but truth be told I probably suffer—and cause more suffering in my loved ones—from undiagnosed, unmedicated attention-deficit, hyperactivity disorder or ADHD. The silence was eating at me, so I decided to edify others. With the greatest of unintended irony, I broke the silence with a random fact for my two older children: "God gave us two ears and just one mouth for a reason." With a half-second delay at most, my quick-witted oldest son, Dane, shot back: "Then you must have two mouths and one ear." The four of us already awake erupted in belly-cramping laughter over that alien image, and, as with all the best humor, the truth it contained. Matthew, the youngest, awoke with a start. So did I, but mine was a different sort of awakening.

As Matthew nodded back off to sleep, and the elder passengers' laughter finally began to subside, I drove deep inside my thoughts. My inner voice pondered not why that was so funny, but why did it also sting so much? The answer was clear: the truth hurts. Just like our body's biological design of nerve endings, our emotional hard wiring is thankfully no different. Pain indicates a wound, and awareness of that wound can lead to healing. Healing occurs if you do something about it. I had let my wound fester for years. I lost track of the number of years in a row that my New Year's resolution was to be a better listener. I thought it was five or six years until I asked my wife. She said, "It's been at least ten years." Then she quickly added, "And I'm still waiting." It stayed on the resolutions list because it never was completed; I had good intentions but poor execution.

I decided on that seven-hour family car ride to do something about it. However, it wasn't until I completed a year-long advanced leadership development program that focused on self-awareness and learning how to listen, that I made sustainable improvement. This powerful training taught me to listen, gave real-life practice opportunities, provided immediate feedback, and left me with additional resources.

A wild approach to leadership is to actively practice listening, and tell people that you are doing exactly that. Then ask for feedback.

Because of decades of bad habits hard to undo, we will always be a work in progress. Maybe your journey as a better listener does not have to be so hard or take as long as mine. Some of us will require professional training to make great strides. I believe we may benefit from ten suggestions I share below. When I finally made meaningful strides as a listener, I experienced the best year of my life. My wife and I enjoyed our closest connection as a married couple, despite our hardest year financially. My adult son became my best buddy, and I became the best man in his wedding. I grew closer with my teenage daughter who comfortably talked with me about her first date. My younger son randomly said to me, after a long time of quietly working side by side in our workshop, "I love you daddy." Oh, how I wish I learned to listen and value quiet time sooner in life! What had I missed over the years? Please do not miss out. I share with you below a helpful product of that productive pain. I learned to...

HOLD THE LANTERN

Film critic Terence Rafferty said, "What you discover on your own is always more exciting than what someone else discovers for you—it's like the difference between romantic love and an arranged marriage." It is not the firm, warm handshake, charming smile, enthusiastic head nod, nor the genuine exclamation, "Yeah, me too!" that will deeply connect you with another person. Excellent listening will forge the strongest bonds and has the great benefit of helping another.

A wild approach to leadership is to be willing to travel down a dark, emotional mine shaft with another, but illuminate the path, not direct it. Hold the lantern, but do not lead the way. A good leader—who is ideally a good listener—will gently guide another to self-discovery.

I developed the "top ten" list below after decades of doing mostly the exact opposite. This list comes after years of mistakes, training, research, and my own experience in trial-and-error. The numbering of a 1-10 reflects that this is generally a stepwise approach, and not in priority order.

1. **Allow a lot of time.** Excellent listening is hard work and takes time. Plan for up to an hour or more for a meaningful conversation. Some personality types take longer to gather thoughts and express them.

2. **Be present.** Your mind and body must be relaxed and free from distractions and obstacles. Come out from behind your desk if you are in your office. Sit on the same side of the table or desk as the other person. Place your phone on silent, and keep a TV or computer screen out of your line of sight. Without being overly intense and creepy about it, mostly look into their eyes.

3. **Anticipate and welcome quiet time.** Long pauses with no words can be productive. Let silence do the heavy lifting. This will be extremely difficult for you extroverts like me, but it gets easier with practice.

4. **Gently prompt if needed and never interrupt.** Say "I hear you," "I understand what you are saying," and know that a slow, gentle head nod with good eye contact is often most effective. In the *Becoming the Totally Responsible Person* the authors say that "Empathy is fostered through silence, listening, observing, and sensitivity to the emotions and thoughts of others."[71]

5. **Now the hard one: do not "rescue" the other person.** Strong emotions may come, including tears, harsh words, and aggressive nonverbal gestures. Steven M.R. Covey advises in *The Speed of Trust* that, "...as long as a person is communicating with high emotion, he or she does not yet feel understood ... A person will usually not ask for your

advice until he or she feels understood."[45] Do not "rescue" the other person from reaching a deeper understanding themselves. Help them have a full experience by *not* offering consoling words. You will pull them back; let them go. Just be there with them in that literal and figurative space. Think of that space as a dark mine shaft they must travel. Their finest "gold nuggets" of truth, realization, and ultimate comfort will usually follow the strong emotions. Travel with them, hold the lantern, but do not lead the way down. Our job is to help illuminate the path, not direct it. The poet Robert Browning Hamilton wrote: "I walked a mile with Pleasure; she chattered all the way; but left me none the wiser for all she had to say. I walked a mile with Sorrow, and ne'er a word said she; But oh! The things I learnt from her when Sorrow walked with me."

6. **Ask questions later.** People often have more to share when you don't interject. Know that once you ask a question or make a comment, you will direct the conversation, however small. Let the conversation unfold at their pace and direction. They will make it known when they are receptive to your questions, comments, or advice. In the book *Helping*, Dr. Edgar H. Schein said: "...engaging in an active but humble inquiry process that 1) keeps clients in the driver's seat to enable them to regain status by becoming active problem solvers on their own behalf, 2) gives them confidence that they can solve their own dilemma to some degree, and 3) reveals as much data as possible for both the client and helper to work with." [20]

7. **Gently ask questions.** Often a simple reflection of their words—rather than a question—is most helpful. It demonstrates that we carefully listened. Phrases such as, "I

13

hear you," "I heard you say…" or a request to "tell me more" will prompt them to go deeper and share further. Asking "how" is powerful and should be used more often than "why" or "because," as they can elicit a defensive response, implying that another must justify their actions or words. "Why" and "because" should be used with great care. Listen for a deeper meaning behind words and listen for what is not being said, the latter may be more obvious to us than them; an outside perspective can be especially illuminative. Lastly, keep our "but" out of it. If we feel like we want to prompt a response with a "but" (which usually has a negative connotation), simply replace it with an "and" (which has a more neutral connotation).

8. **Do not make light of another's concerns or suggest how they should feel.** If your response to their concern would sound anything like, "well, at least …" or "look on the bright side" then stay silent. One of the least productive things is to say how another should feel. Instead, help them deal with their feelings, mostly by being present and providing an ear. No amount of convincing by you can sway another if they don't believe it themselves; they must see and decide for themselves. In *A Long Obedience in the Same Direction*, Eugene H. Peterson says that, "We need an eye specialist rather than, say, a painter. A painter tries to convey to us with the aid of his brush and palette a picture of the world as he sees it; an ophthalmologist tries to enable us to see the world as it really is."[66] Drawn from a little research and a whole lot of mistakes I've made over the years; below are six things you would not want to say and six things that are usually helpful to say.

9. **Do not share your story.** Your story is often irrelevant and usually does more harm than good. Among the worst things you can say is, "Well, when I was your age..." or "What I would do if I were you is..." Newsflash: You are likely not her age, and you are not him. You do have not have her unique genetic makeup, experienced life as him, nor are living in her or his present situation. When first meeting someone and in light conversation a well-intended comparison such as "Oh, yeah. Me too!" and "I can totally relate to that," will enable a pleasant surface connection between people. However, that approach will often repel deeper conversation and connection. Keep it about them until they ask about you. Take the advice of actor Lisa Kirk who said, "A gossip is one who talks to you about another; a bore is one who talks to you about himself; and a brilliant conversationalist is one who talks to you about yourself."

10. **Check your assumptions, your intentions, and then speak...*maybe*.** We carry our assumptions with us at all times, and we add to them as we listen to others unless we ask clarifying questions. Well-placed questions will help you understand a situation better and enable other persons to improve their own understanding. When you are ready to provide your perspective—if it is even necessary at all—

do so only after checking your intentions. Ask yourself, "Does what I'm about to say have the other's best interest in mind?" The old saying, "sticks and stones may break my bones, but words will never hurt me" has it backwards. Physical wounds heal relatively quickly; emotional damage often lasts a lifetime. The Apostle Paul advises to, "…not let any unwholesome talk come out of your mouths, but only what is helpful for building others up according to their needs, that it may benefit those who listen." Note that it is not a suggestion to say only nice things. We should strive to be kind, not just nice. Niceness is politeness, rarely getting to truth. Kindness demands that at times we share painful, frank feedback with the best intentions for another's well-being. Speak if it might help illuminate something for the other person but share your thoughts only after first considering the impact of your words. If you're like me, over-explaining is a weakness. Off-the-cuff and less thoughtful word choices can confuse or offend the listener before you even reach your main point.

Excellent listening will take practice, as you will have years of old habits to break. While writing this book, and, in fact, just a few weeks after I finished the section above on listening, I blew it again. A work colleague, normally quite stoic, shed tears after sharing how on-going marital troubles affected her ability to make a career move. My second in command at the time—who I'd be wise to follow more of the time—stayed quiet, and carefully listened for more to be said. However, I interjected. I said something along the lines of, "we totally understand; don't worry about the career. Your marriage comes first. Your work will always be there. You are well thought of and there will be lots of opportunities in the future." Those were kind words to be sure. However, consider my deputy's approach, far more effective than mine. He seemed to ignore my ramble, remained fixed on our colleagues' eyes, stayed quiet a moment longer, and then offered, softly, "I am so sorry. My heart breaks for you." I knew once again; I am a work in progress.

Anticipate two steps forward and ask forgiveness when you take a step in the wrong direction. Regularly seek feedback, and you may experience the kind of life-changing results I shared in the first section of this chapter. Sometimes a connection comes easy and the way to resolve an issue is obvious, and sometimes it's very hard work. This is because sometimes...

IT'S NEVER ABOUT WHAT THEY SAY

I suppressed what really troubled me the day I came closest to big trouble at work. As a young manager I was invited to attend a meeting that my boss helped his boss organize. The meeting was for our national leader to hear from field managers from across the region. The meeting started early, and by lunchtime, all the national leader had done was talk. When others spoke, he interrupted them. The fourth time he did it, I slammed my half-eaten pizza down into the box. and topped it off with a loud, sarcastic remark.

After the meeting, my supervisor pulled me aside. Though I knew I had it coming, my boss (and a mentor to this day) didn't let me have it. Instead, he simply asked if I was okay. He said my behavior was unlike me. His inexplicable compassion led me to quickly get past my annoyance with the national chief and get to the heart of the matter: my wife had a miscarriage two days prior.

A wild approach to leadership is to know that people are never most upset about what they say they are upset about. Really? Never? No, never. I try to prove that wrong, but never can.

Are people usually mad about what say they are mad about? No. There's always more to it, and often something surprisingly unrelated.

For example, one day my daughter Taylor walked toward my wife and I with tears in her eyes, still thinking about an argument she had earlier that day...or so we thought. As my wife and I listened, it became clear to us that Taylor was more upset about the long Christmas break ending and school starting the next day. But then we *really* listened: we kept our mouths shut and allowed time for our daughter's thoughts and words to unfold. We learned that what troubled Taylor more deeply was the uncertainty of where she would go to college the next fall and the sadness that her childhood was over. Following my wife's lead (which almost always tends to work better), we continued to stay silent and pay attention. Taylor later thanked us, and said she was grateful we just listened and did not provide any unsolicited advice.

The authors of *The Practice of Adaptive Leadership* said, "Look for the body language, eye contact, emotion, energy...pay as much attention to what is not being said as you do what is being said."[22] In *The Richest Man Who Ever Lived* Steven K. Scott wrote: "Arguments are often started not because they're necessary, but because one party is angry. And more times than not, this anger has nothing to do with the argument."[41]

We learned that Taylor only wanted to express herself and know that someone cared. We also were reminded that what we think is bothering someone is almost never what they say. It may be easier for us to listen and deeply connect with family members like Taylor, but what about work colleagues? How do we connect with them? The answer may surprise you. It requires us to...

18

BE MORE THAN A FRIEND

"Familiarity breeds contempt" is an old saying. It suggests that the more people get to know us, the less they will respect, appreciate, or want to follow us. You were probably taught not get too close to your employees or the team you lead. I was. We were told that if you get emotionally attached to your team members, they either won't respect you or it will be too hard to counsel or discipline them if they have performance or conduct issues. My three decades of work experience as a supervisor, manager, and leader, and, more importantly, research, shows this is simply not true.

The more people get to know us—and we get to know them—trust builds, and a stronger relationship develops. In the book *The Work of Leaders* the authors wrote: "In 1968, University of Michigan psychologist Robert Zajonc began a series of landmark experiments showing that, contrary to the old saying, familiarity does not breed contempt. In fact, just the opposite is true. People's feelings, even toward nonsensical words, consistently grow more positive as their exposure increases." [53]

So, as trust builds in a leader, people are more likely to follow. That said, when is it that we cross the line of friendly relationships with those that we lead? When is our personal connection inappropriate? Doesn't the leader need to maintain some emotional distance? Aside from any sort of romantic relationship—which is always inappropriate in boss-employee roles—the answer may surprise you, and it's very simple: be more than just a friend.

A wild approach to leadership is to love work colleagues like family. Give your team all your heart. John P. Kotter writes, "For centuries we have heard the expression, 'Great leaders win over the hearts and minds of others.' The heart comes first...if you want to win over another person, first win his heart, and the rest of him is likely to follow." [40] Let your words and actions demonstrate that you want the very best for them. Treat people fairly. But like your loved ones, don't treat all people the same. Adjust your approach to their unique needs. Praise publicly without hesitation but be equally quick to privately counsel when needed.

This approach goes up the chain as well as down. The concept of loving those you work with like family applies not only to those you lead, but to those who lead you. Love your boss like you love your team. Clay Scroggins writes in *How to Lead When You're Not in Charge*: "You don't necessarily need to like your boss…But you need to choose to love your boss. Loving your boss means you genuinely want what's best for them and you're trying to do what's in their best interests." Scroggins goes on to write that, "One of the greatest difficulties in challenging up is learning to challenge the process without appearing to challenge the person."[63] Building on that advice, it is critical to understand how people best receive feedback. If you are aware of another's personality type, temperament, or style preference, you will be more effective in communications. Using the DISC assessment example, you can be more direct with a "D" or Dominant type person, but it is critical to first make the "C" or cautious type feel safe. This stuff is real. My son Dane is a "D" and if I don't make my point quick, clear, concise, and compelling—or if I dilute my point with too gentle a delivery—he will assume I don't feel strongly about what I'm saying, or he will think I don't have my act together. This approach is in direct contrast to my interactions with my wife, Mary, a cautious "C", and my daughter, Taylor, a supportive "S." With them I am more effective when I slowly and gently approach a subject and courteously explain a point I am trying to make or a position I would like them to understand. With Dane, it's not soft and slow; it's fast and firm—exact opposite approach to get the same, desired result!

Why is it that at work we hesitate to counsel others, yet at home or with loved ones we rarely pause a moment to address issues we have?

We fool ourselves in thinking that "oh, it's not my place…I may have read the situation wrong…it is probably just me…" If you're like me, you once thought that if you brought up anything negative in a mid-year or year-end performance review, or if too many times during the year you focused on a mistake that was made, that you would undermine all the good things the employee was doing.

But the real answer why we don't address more problems with our teams is, in short, we don't care enough. But we must. Dr. John Maxwell tells us in *The 360 Degree Leader*, "When you don't want to have a difficult conversation, you need to ask yourself: 'Is it because it will hurt them, or it will hurt me?' If it is because it will hurt you, then you're being selfish." [50] Maxwell went on to say that, "Good leaders get past the discomfort of having difficult conversations for the sake of the people they lead and the organization." John Piper, author of *Don't Waste Your Life*, wrote that we are taught in a thousand ways that love means increasing someone's self-esteem, helping someone feel good about themselves. Then Piper pivoted and said that's wrong: "Love is doing what's best for someone."[6]

My surface-level, happy-go-lucky traits that made me a great team member and candidate for leadership were the biggest impediment to my actual management and leadership effectiveness once I was in charge. I am a survivor of abuse and alcoholism in my extended family. On top of that, every personality or style assessment I ever took suggested I was hard-wired at birth to be either people-focused or likeability-driven. Therefore, yours truly spent all of his childhood and much of his early adult years always soothing tensions, bringing people together and, sadly, avoiding conflict. Much of the conflict could have been healthy, and if allowed to play out, would have made me, another, or our team stronger.

After many years of seeing conflict-avoidance never work out well long-term—and after much training, coaching, and counseling—I am pleased to say that my growth in conflict resolution has been my greatest personal advancement. No coincidence, it directly corresponded to my greatest professional advancement. One strategy that helps me, which I suggest you try, is to repeat the following before initiating needed conflict:

> *Remember that my desire to comfort them is really a longing to be safe and comforted myself. I must recognize and embrace the value of conflict. The ultimate safety and comfort come from hearing and sharing truth. I choose not to believe the lie that sharing the truth will make people mad, not like me, and create an unsafe situation. Research shows that just the opposite is true. We will all be stronger after healthy conflict.*

To want the best for others, regardless of how it impacts us, is a most powerful approach to life and leadership. To do so, it helps to be secure ourselves, but it is imperative that we create a safe environment for those we lead. We must ensure...

SAFETY FIRST

Question: Why take time to listen longer and deeper when you're busy? Answer: You're actually wasting your time if you don't. It even takes the bluntest and brief among us a while to get to the real heart of the "what's-the-matter." At our innermost core we want to feel safe. This is a need more fundamental to our well-being than to feel loved and know that our life matters. If made to feel safe and given the opportunity, others will share far more than you ever imagined. Your relationships will improve; thus your leadership influence will grow. Your team's performance will also improve. The authors of *Think Again* noted that, "Psychologically safe teams reported more errors ... (and) ... actually made fewer errors. By freely admitting their mistakes, they were then able to learn what had caused them and eliminate them moving forward."[74] They also cited a study at Google which discovered that the most important difference wasn't who was on the team or even how meaningful their work was. What mattered most was psychological safety. What is psychological safety? Again, from *Think Again*: "psychological safety is not a matter of relaxing standards, making people feel comfortable, being nice and agreeable, or giving unconditional praise. It's fostering a climate of respect, trust, and openness in which people can raise concerns and suggestions without fear of reprisal. It's the foundation of a learning culture."

I served as a coach at a year-long advanced leadership development program. There were 24 up-and-coming enrollees. A student, who I'll call Rochelle, wanted to share her frustrating need to be hyper-organized in order to be effective. Well, that's what she said she wanted to talk about. Knowing that she seemed emotionally disconnected during the early weeks of the program, I took extra care to listen carefully to her and demonstrate my genuine interest and concern. Then, when Rochelle felt she was in a safe space with me, she shared—literally out of the blue—that her parents rarely told her they loved her. She cried for some time, and, after that, she engaged more personally and deeply in the program, embracing a lot of the teachings and strategies to improve her leadership. Her professional growth, up through a promotion, was quite evident in the first two years. Later, a few check-in phone calls with her made clear her personal life benefitted as well. Glad I listened for a change.

I heard Paul Jeremy coming long before he reached my door. His footsteps were more like foot stomps, in spite of his slender build. I was later told that along the long hallway that led to my office, loose papers flew off cubicle desks in the wind wake of his walk while heads popped out of several offices wondering what Paul was mad about this time…and curious how I, the young, new regional chief would handle him. Paul Jeremy was close to retirement and infamous in the office for explosive behavior at times. He often spoke loudly, quickly, and interrupted others—and that's when he was in a good mood. This time Paul was mad. His pace quickened as he approached my office door, which he then slammed so hard that the clock on the wall crashed to the floor. Seeming indifferent to the literal mess he just made as he stepped over rolling clock parts, Paul exploded about a figurative mess he perceived in the office. To this day, I do not recall the substance of his initial rant, but I do remember how my heart raced, my eyebrows dropped, my eyes narrowed, and my face reddened. I then remember—surprised still today as I was then—my inexplicable restraint and wise choice in that moment: I just listened. Though I wanted to yell: "Who the heck are you to come into my office, your boss's boss, unannounced, slam the door, raise your voice…" But for some reason I didn't. I just listened and invited Paul to sit next to me.

About two minutes into his ramble and midway through one of his many sentences devoid of a period (and barely a comma), Paul nearly yelled, "and you didn't even ask me about my heart attack." Then he continued with his initial complaint. Then it struck me; the lightbulb appeared over my head. "Ah-ha, now *that's* it" I thought. I was grateful I just listened further and didn't chime in with, "Ask you?! Heck, I can't even get one word in!"

No one had known about Paul's heart attack, how scared he was, nor how bad he was hurting. I was just glad that I didn't prompt another heart attack by way of a shouting match. I felt blessed to be there for this man who was scared and confused. I exhaled long and slowly, and when he finally paused a few minutes later, I said, "Paul, tell me about your heart attack." I don't recall how we wrapped up that conversation, but I do know that on the way back to his office he told several people, that, "The new young guy is going to be alright!"

Others will forget the details of your decisions over time—the logic that appealed to the head has a shorter memory. However, people will never forget how we made them feel.

The Heart Never Forgets is more than just a song title by LeAnn Rimes. It's a universal truth. Do you make others feel vulnerable, cautious, neglected—or safe, trusted, valued? Megan Reitz and John Higgins wrote in the Harvard Business Review: "If you are wondering why others aren't speaking up more, first ask yourself how you are inadvertently silencing them." [31] When safe, your leaders, managers, supervisors, and their employees will more openly express their diverse viewpoints, which will ultimately strengthen decisions. It's more important to hear the "no" and "maybe" from your staff, than the "probably" and the "yes." In the words of Barry Rand of Xerox, "If you have a yes-man working for you, one of you is redundant." The stakes are too high for redundancy in most organizations. So let us remember to make others feel safe, and a big part of that is to stay under control. When I stayed calm, I helped Paul to calm down. And I learned to…

ACTUALLY CALM DOWN

Do you want to try an experiment? It will have predictable results, no matter who you try it on. Next time someone is very upset, tell them, with no other instruction, to "calm down!" You don't even have to yell it for the experiment to work; just say it. Here's the thing though: it never works. Have you ever noticed how a yawn is contagious, how we tend to talk fast when others are talking fast, or how we scratch an itch that wasn't there the moment before we saw someone else scratch their itch first?

I used to *yell* "calm down!" when I was a federal game warden, going after poachers; when I tried to settle down young athletes on the youth sports teams I coached, and—with the worst results of all—when I tried it with my teenage children. "Calm down!" never suddenly relaxes anyone. Most get more upset by that instruction. What does work for us? A slow deep breath followed by a soft low voice. Like the mimic of an itch or a yawn, they almost always will follow suit. It's like magic. Stacy Armitage, an excellent leader, friend, and former teacher said: "I found nothing quieted my classroom down more quickly than me whispering in the front of the room. If I yelled or raised my voice the class typically just got louder."

Once we literally and figuratively turn down the volume, word choice is essential to create a safe environment to connect with others. Though actions speak louder than words, words have weight.

The saying, "Sticks and stones may break my bones but words will never hurt me" is wrong. Emotional wounds often last longer than physical ones.

It has been said that "laughter is the best medicine." That may be true most of the time, but it can be poison some of the time. The use of humor in the middle of a crucial conversation can distract and minimize the impact of our words. It was early in my boss Matt's tenure, and we did not yet have a strong rapport. I noticed he was never a passenger, only the driver, on several work trips. Bob asked to drive, and Matt said, "nah, I've got it." I whimsically said, "Don't bother asking. Matt is a control freak." Matt's reaction told me I had better explain myself (Good thing I didn't next tell Matt to "calm down!"). I learned that the use of humor in this case was an underhanded, passive-aggressive way to make a point. Not at all passive-aggressive I would tell my children to…

GO TO YOUR ROOM!

Before I learned to stay calm and listen, I would command my oldest child: "Go to your room!" Dane would then march down the hall and shut his door. "Go in time out!" was my instruction to our next child, with the thought I had developed a more advanced approach. Taylor would then sit cross-legged in the hallway halfway between the kitchen entry and the AC vent. "Well, I showed them," I convinced myself, having achieved the silence I demanded as as a result of their insolence. At the time I reasoned that I was at least better than our parents, who might slap us across the face.

So, what did I just teach my children? The way to solve problems is to let the authoritative figure have the last word, go separate ways, not resolve anything, and stay silent.

The version of that we bring to work as a boss doesn't work any better either. While we often have a chance to repair a damaged parent-child relationship, if we shut down our employees as we do our children, we will not get their best energies and ideas. At worst, if we continue a "go to your room!" approach as a supervisor, our employee might quit and never come back. Let us try a wildly different approach to parent or lead a team. Let us follow the example of a native culture in Canada who discovered another way. Rather than shut their children up, "The Cree do the opposite; they bring the child into a family circle and let him 'talk out' his frustrations," writes Dr. Steven R. Covey in *The 3rd Alternative*.[47]

In my experience with the Cree's approach to parenting— which I regrettably did not learn until my older two were teenagers— it worked better every time. Not *nearly* every time. *Every* time. The Cree approach can work at work and with our other teams as well, and it does not mean that we don't later address people's bad behavior.

This "be-in" to get "buy-in" will result in more ownership of the solution.

It means only that we first hold our words to let them share theirs initially, and in doing so, learn more about the overall context of the situation. This will help calibrate appropriate consequences. More importantly, we create an environment for others to recognize their error themselves. Exhibiting that patience and extending that trust, as difficult as it is, will also boost morale. Harder still is to…

TRUST WHEN IT DOESN'T MAKE SENSE

Ronald Reagan famously said, "Trust, but verify." I say to that: "Mr. President: that is not trust. That is suspicion." It is disingenuous at best—if not dishonest—to lead another to believe we trust them when we do not. Imagine our team members' range of reactions— hurt feelings, sapped morale, and then a lack of trust in us—when they learn that we went behind their back to verify something. We are served better to follow the advice of Ralph Waldo Emerson: "Trust (people) and they will be true to you; treat them greatly and they will show themselves great." A wild approach to leadership is to trust when it doesn't make sense—trust almost everyone nearly all the time. If we trust when it doesn't make sense, we will be disappointed from time to time. That's manageable.

What's unmanageable is to constantly replace team members who leave, uncomfortable in a culture of suspicion—undervalued and untrusted.

Wally Bock writes that we should make it easy for the good guys. "Too many processes seem like they're designed to make sure that nobody puts anything over on the company. The fact is most of the people…try to do the right thing. Make it easy for them…have auditors check up on things and catch the people who are abusing the system. Then deal with them accordingly. In the meantime, the good folks will be happier and more productive, and you'll be more profitable."[14] For those we have not yet established trust, we may want to say: "I appreciate what you've shared with me. I will gather some additional information, and I will get back with you." For all others, especially your team members who should be fully trusted (or they should not be on your team), let us adopt an innocent until proven guilty mindset.

I wish I did a couple things differently when my children were teenagers, especially around being a better listener. One thing their mother and I got more right than wrong related to trust. Extending trust was more difficult with cars and curfews, but it was most critical then because those things mattered most. We told our children when they first earned their driver's license that they had our trust to obey traffic laws and arrive home by their curfew after evening sporting events or visits to friends' houses; we would be asleep and see them in the morning. We told them they had our full trust—no suspicion, no verification, and no explanations needed—unless they broke our trust. As I write this years later, none of our children ever had a traffic ticket (In contrast, I had six speeding tickets before I turned 24). Our adult children told us later that they would not only get home by their curfew, but they would also often arrive a few minutes earlier to ensure our trust was not broken with them.

In contrast, we have friends who question their children about underage drinking, who stay awake just to see if their kids get home on time, and allow them a cell phone only if they are able to track their whereabouts electronically. Our friends' children would then tell my wife and I that they felt as if they were guilty until proven innocent. So, no surprise, some have drunk underage, snuck out and snuck home late, and found ways around cell phone tracking to keep their whereabouts unknown to their parents. I have coached hundreds of young people in sports. Many have told me that at school and home if they are regularly accused of something they didn't do, they might as well do it and at least have some fun.

There is an alternative: trust. Grant others a good reputation to live up to, then watch them shine. When you do, you'll find that...

WHAT COMES AROUND GOES AROUND

My research shows that the phrase, "what comes around goes around," was first penned in 1974 by author Eddie Stone. I first heard those words a decade later as a teenager courtesy rock band Ratt's hit song *Round and Round.* The concept really struck me though the first and only time I tried to play tetherball alone. How quickly and painfully some things set in motion come back around. Most things we plant as leaders take years to harvest, but sometimes we reap returns rather rapidly.

On my Delta airlines flight from Atlanta, Georgia, to Little Rock, Arkansas, I was unexpectedly upgraded to first-class seating. For some reason, I was not thinking of myself first that day as I usually would, and instead gave my luxury, first-class plane seat to my team member, Mindy Gautreaux, who had worked particularly long hours that week. As we boarded, she said that this would be her first time in first class, and then added that it was her birthday, also news to me. As Mindy slid into her cushy seat and thanked me once more, I negotiated the narrow aisle down towards the crowded, noisier end of the plane. However, that day—and not by coincidence I remain convinced—I had an aisle all to myself. I spread out comfortably in the middle of three vacant seats, as if I were in first class. Meanwhile, Mindy told the airline steward what I had done for her, and the entire flight crew then treated me like I was first class, complete with extra drinks and the variety of snacks elegantly placed in the weaved basket normally reserved for the folks up front.

The best definition of love that I can come up with is this: Love is wanting the best for another regardless how it impacts us.

Thinking of others first—loving others—is the right thing to do. It's also the smart thing: what comes around goes around.

It can be a hard thing, but author and speaker Bob Goff reminds us that learning to love will always be a work in progress. Goff calls it "becoming love" and took it a step further in his book, *Everybody Always*: "Loving people we don't understand or agree with is just the kind of beautiful, counterintuitive, risky stuff people who are becoming love do."[72].

I like to say that when we are learning to love we should *verb* our way to the *noun*. That is, we do love to have love, and give away our time, talent, and treasure. In the movie *Dear John*, actor Channing Tatum's character sells his entire treasure—his coin collection worth tens of thousands of dollars—to anonymously pay for his ex-girlfriend's new husband's cancer treatment. That's love. Maybe you don't go to that length; I'm not sure I would. But we can.

When we do for others, good will seems to always come back to us in some form. We all need all the help we can get from one another, because this life is hard. Life is hard from the start, and it doesn't get easier because...

THE CHILD IS FATHER TO THE MAN

Say what? Poet William Wordsworth used that phrase to mean that the influences of childhood greatly affect our lives long into adulthood. My dad died of cancer when he was 63. I still carry a regret today from a single sentence he uttered that I left unaddressed.

During his last six months, Dad and I often sat alone together on his back porch. We talked mostly of the present. We discussed tools in the shop, birds in the bird feeder, and, of course, the weather, avoiding what mattered most, the rich details from the past. There was one moment, however, when he said, in his thick, deep Brooklyn, New York accent, "I keep havin' dees *dawts*." Then he quickly got quiet again as if awaiting a response. Did I say, "What *thoughts* are you having, dad? Talk to me. Please tell me what's haunting you." No, I didn't, and it remains one of my deepest regrets. Instead, I sat beside him in silence.

I desperately wanted to know what thoughts he was talking about, but I didn't ask. I froze in fear, too scared of where that question might lead us.

Had I asked my dad about his "dawts" that day, he might have opened up and said that he wished he could have been there for me emotionally, but that it was just too hard for him. He might also have gone on to express the things I most needed to hear. "You know, son, you were a great kid. The divorce wasn't your fault. Though I had to leave, I am so sorry I hurt you. I loved you so much then, and I do now. I just want you to know that." My dad might have really needed to say that and I really needed to hear it. Even as a grown man with children of my own, I still do. The thing is, I will never know what he wanted to say.

I made a choice to use that regret to inspire a new response when I sense that a person is mad, sad, or otherwise has a troubling thought. Using my dad's word "dawts," I rely on my new acronym, D-A-W-T, to challenge me to Dare to Ask What's Troubling. Now, I summon the courage to gently press with words and phrases such as, "Tell me more … because? … How is that?" We don't need a prepared speech or to speak much at all. It's usually best to sit quietly and simply listen.

What I allowed to happen to me does not have to happen to you. Listen carefully to loved ones, friends, and others in need. At minimum you might miss a good laugh, a cold beer, a great story, or maybe you will have a good cry and heal a long-held wound. The stakes could be even higher. Perhaps you might keep someone out of prison, save a marriage, and even save a life. I heard more than one story about someone who decided not to die by suicide after a complete stranger was kind or a friend just called and listened. A deep connection to others in leadership and life itself leads to influence, productivity, and happiness. To strengthen our work with others, we must first start with work on ourselves. That's where we go next.

CHAPTER 2

Character — Work On Ourselves

INTRODUCTION

N ow we begin the work on the most important and most challenging subject: you...and me. If this book must be limited to just one chapter, this would be the one. To effectively lead others, we must first lead ourselves well. If we could get one thing right to be a better leader, it is to develop and maintain strong character. The rest of this book and the limit of our leadership depends upon and builds off character—what we are made of or what we make of ourselves. Integrity and character are often used interchangeably. I define integrity as the outward expression of character. That is, our words and actions match our beliefs. Andy Stanley says that integrity is doing what you ought to do even if it costs you. With integrity, people will trust us to have good intentions and get things done—a leader worthy of trust and followers. However, a good reputation can collapse with a serious lapse in integrity. Widely respected billionaire Warren Buffett said, "It takes twenty years to build a reputation and five minutes to ruin it...I look for three things in hiring people. The first is personal integrity, the second is intelligence, and the third is a high energy level. But, if you don't have the first, the other two will kill you."

More than 200 years before Buffet, General George Washington, given an army largely of untrained farmers and tradesmen, had to limit his focus to what mattered most. He wrote, "I can answer but for three things: a firm belief in the justice of our cause; close attention in the prosecution of it; and the strictest integrity."[42]

A wide array of personalities and leadership styles are effective, and a leader's flexibility is essential. However, to not compromise our moral convictions—our structural integrity if you will—is critical. If we can agree that we must lead *within* ourselves well, we might consider that leadership is both an internal structure and an external structure. Picture the world-famous Eiffel tower in Paris, France. No matter how cleverly arranged the 7,000 metric tons of iron pieces are—their connections and collaborations if you will—without a solid foundation the Eiffel tower would collapse under the first significant outside pressure. So goes our leadership if our foundation and structure is not firm. Across the English Channel from the Eiffel Tower, British statesman John Morley said that "No man can climb out beyond the limitations of his own character." We remove limits on effective leadership when we solidify our foundation; that of character.

Character, like leadership overall, is developed through time, built on mistakes made and lessons learned.

Character development is a process of adaptive learning and not the product of birth. Dr. Steven Covey said in *Principle-Centered Leadership* that "I am not a product of my culture, my conditioning, and the conditions of my life; rather, I am a product of my value system, attitudes, behaviors—and those things I control."[49] On that hopeful note, we build the muscles for long strides in leadership growth only after we master the finer motor skills of self-awareness, the basis of

36

self-leadership. The first commandment of leadership is to know thyself. So...

"COME IN AND KNOW ME BETTER, MAN!"

A wild approach to leadership is to follow in the footsteps of Ebenezer Scrooge.

"Come in...and know me better, man! I am the Ghost of Christmas Present. Look upon me! You have never seen the like of me before!" Ebenezer Scrooge received this invitation from the Ghost of Christmas Present in the Charles Dickens classic *A Christmas Carol.*[62] Scrooge learned in a wink that this was no visit to acquaint with a Ghost, rather a journey to discover self, beginning with his present impact on others, for better—or as in the case of Scrooge—for worse.

Combined with memories of Christmas Past and the potential forecast of Christmas Future, Scrooge's journey of self-discovery and awareness became a timeless classic. From 1843 in leather bound print, the story would be retold by radio broadcast in the late 1800s, performed on Broadway in the early 1900s, appeared in musical form on Hollywood movie screen courtesy the Muppets in the late 1900s, and was streamed on hand-held devices in a drama starring Jim Carrey in the early 2000s. Why does the story survive across three centuries? Because it is the story of you and the story of me. To "Come in... and know me better..." is what each of us desperately needs to grow our leadership.

Personal growth and leadership development programs starts with self: self-discovery and self-awareness. It is an honest conversation with you about me. As Ann Landers advised, "Don't accept your dog's admiration as conclusive evidence that you are wonderful." Our growth continues with an honest conversation with others about us. We work from the inside out.

It starts with us about us. A friend can help us see a blind spot, but not always help see the inside. My oldest son, Dane, a leader of hundreds of adults and youth, wrote: "Even though we know what's going on inside us better than anyone else, the people we are closest with know how we come across better than we do." We have blind spots, so a deeper dive into self will require some independent study. If I may be your professor for a moment, your first assignment will include all *F's*. You won't fail though if you reflect on *family, friends, faith, fun,* and *fears* through the following *who, what, when, where, why,* and *how* questions listed below. After each question, close your eyes, and reflect for a moment:

1. *Who does your family and friends count on?*
2. *What is your hope in?*
3. *When do you experience real joy?*
4. *Where do your fears come from?*
5. *Why do those fears limit you?*
6. *How have you excelled in the past?*

So, do you perceive yourself as an ill-tempered Scrooge or feel like easy-going Bob Cratchit? Did you struggle with one or more of the six questions as I did? There are answers to all those questions. You will know them in time if you learn the *real* you and how you *really* come across to others—and then what to do about it. The latter will grow you most as a healthy person and effective leader.

Luckily nowadays there is an ever-increasing number of assessments that enable you to know thyself better. Depending upon which personality test we take, we may learn if our temperament is red, yellow, green or blue; if we function as ESTJ or INFP; whether we default to executor, refiner, creator, or advancer; or if we are likeability, significance, or competency driven. These assessments can be exhausting and enlightening all at once. They are helpful to us individually, and when worked through with others, can provide a common language and understanding to improve group dynamics. When the assessments include our own input as well as the anonymous input of others, they are particularly powerful. We obtain insights into these questions: What is our innate wiring? What are our deeper needs? What do we need to develop or grow?

I offer two cautions after two decades' worth of personal experiences with a variety of personality tests:

(1) Take several assessments because each one is like a puzzle piece that when looked at alone can leave us guessing. However, when connected with other pieces, the picture of who we are becomes larger and clearer. If the puzzle analogy does not resonate, consider them tools: pliers, hammer, screwdriver, wrench, and saw. When used independently, each tool has an application and can be helpful. However, when used collectively as a cohesive set carried together in a toolbox, almost anything can be fixed, restored, or enhanced. One last analogy: each assessment is a different window view through the house that is me and you. Certain tests provide a better view into certain rooms. Additional tests provide a more complete picture of our internal layout.

(2) More importantly, let no assessment nor other person define who we are or what we can be. We are far more complex, flexible, and resilient than any one assessment or group of them can ascribe. The best instructors help walk students through personality, style, or temperament assessments and teach that we have myriad abilities and can flex our talents as needed.

When we have done all that exhausting work, let us give ourselves an actual and then a figurative break. All we can do is that which is in our span of control. We cover that next.

THE BEST VERSION OF YOU

I once had six older brothers. Erik, my biological brother, was unlike our three foster brothers who left early or the two stepbrothers who came later. Erik was the constant, and I constantly tried to be like him. My dad left us the first time when I was just six, so Erik, more than five years my elder, was the closest thing I had to my role model. I would lay on my belly on our kitchen floor, one eye on my Matchbox cars and the other eye on Erik. I would watch and follow him. He would open the screen door to go in the backyard, and I would follow so fast that the door he just opened would close behind me untouched. Erik would get on his bike; I would jump on mine. He would hop the fence to play in the woods; I would throw one leg over and be just a few steps behind. Sometimes he invited me. I wanted to do what Erik did and be who Erik was. The problem for me was, Erik is literally a genius. I could only follow him so far. He spoke in adult-like sentences when he was 18 months old, read by age 3, and is now a college professor. Clearly, I had to find my own way. It took a while through the teen and early adult years. I later gained assurance from C.S Lewis: "We see only the results which a man's choices make out of his raw material. But God does not judge him on the raw material at all, but on what he has done with it." [2] I then wrote down these six words that changed my paradigm forever: *become...the best version...of you.*

> *become*............we are all, always a work in progress
> *the best version*...............improve on what we have
> *of you*.............work on us, not compare us to others

I gained further comfort when I read Andy Stanley, leadership expert and author of dozens of books, say: "Look to others for inspiration (but) not imitation...Compare yourself to who you were yesterday, not who someone else is today."

So, be the best version of you. Consider that it's not the level you've achieved in life that matters, rather your progress made in getting there. We all grow from different starting points in life and end up in different places. This is a result of an infinitely unique combination of gifts and challenges we were born with, challenges and blessings since birth, and our own hard work. So don't be so hard on yourself, but you are this far in this book for a reason: you want to grow as a person and become a better leader. We all have our issues to work on, and we first must...

NAME IT TO TAME IT

I talk a lot. This I know, for my family tells me so.

Something I did not know, though, until recently was that I was not open to conversations about deeper fears and other feelings. Apparently, to speak up and to open up are not the same thing. I also learned later in life that I have a need for control. How did I learn these things, and how can you, too?

- *self-assessments* – take several of them for different viewpoints as discussed above.
- *counseling* – there's no shortage of good counselors and many are free.
- *training* – in-person courses can be especially powerful with group interactions.
- *independent study* – there's no shortage of books on leadership and other self-help.
- *mentoring* – have a mentor and be a mentor.

41

- *experience* – experience, bad as well as good, can be our best teacher.
- *ask others* – (that's the focus of our next section)

I learned through the methods above, especially good counseling, that I wouldn't let people get to know me at a deep level. This is because my primary motivation is control. Though my desire for control helps during unorganized meetings or stressful situations where prompt leadership is needed, it can also harm personal relationships and disempower and demoralize staff.

My need for control is rooted in wiring from birth and also a desire for safety because of tragic incidents in my early childhood. Before I was eight years old, I experienced my parents' nasty separation then divorce, endured abuse, and my best friend was killed when hit by a car. Those experiences caused my struggles. What are yours? We all have them. Many of us wrestle with peace, perfection, popularity, or power. Know this: there is a reason you do what you do. Like every trait we have—most given to us without our permission through nature or early nurture—can be managed for our good fortune and for the benefit of others. This positive turn will only happen, however, if we are aware of it. We can only make strides if we know what we do, why we do it, and what to do with that knowledge.

Fortunately, there are many tools to help us look deeper into ourselves, including our subconscious to gain *insight*—literally *sight into* you and me—to grow our leadership.

We have to name it to tame it. Those around us can help if we let them, but it can sting at times. A wild approach to leadership is to...

HURT YOUR OWN FEELINGS...

I jammed my car in park at the red traffic light. My heart raced. I fumbled with nervous hands to log into my phone and open the email I saw at the last stoplight. The subject line read something like, "Confidential Instructor Feedback." The week before I was a new, one-time instructor at a national training center. I prepared for weeks to deliver a one-hour session on career development. I thought my heart would soar when I read the anonymous student survey about me. What I read, however, broke my heart.

A wild approach to leadership is to take the famous fitness phrase, "no pain, no gain," and apply it to your emotional health and not just your physical pursuits. The saying, "the truth hurts" is only accurate when we *know* the truth. Try hard to get your feelings hurt. It will be effective 100% of the time, even for those who are tough, emotionally detached, or just more stoic than the rest of us. You may have heard the old adage, "What doesn't kill you makes you stronger." I would add four essential words on the end of that sentence to make it true: "...if you let it." When we ask others for honest feedback about our weaknesses and strengths, we will get our feelings hurt, even if just a little. There will be pain, but here will be gain.

The anonymous feedback I received as an instructor did break my heart. In fact, I felt my heart stop when I read the first comment. Why did it hurt so badly? Two reasons: I cared, and it was accurate. Students wrote that I came across as a 31-year-old know-it-all, that I dove into the material too soon, and that I never connected with my audience. Twenty years later, do you know what I do every single time I speak to a new audience? I ask about them; I tell my story, especially the part about a tough upbringing; and I make time to build rapport and trust.

Receiving in-person, face-to-face feedback is a wildly difficult approach to learn, but we will improve with time and practice. Instead,

43

or preferably in addition, ask for written feedback we well. The two together will be powerful. It will allow the feedback provider to think more deeply and present feedback more thoughtfully. Written feedback can come in the form of on-line "360-degree" evaluations. However, what I found most helpful is to ask my bosses, my employees, and my colleagues the three simple questions that follow. The questions are phrased to enable the feedback providers to be feel more comfortable than if we asked them to do a numeric rating or to tell us what we do well versus where we need to improve. Simply ask:

1. What should I start doing that I'm not doing now?

2. What should I stop doing?

3. What should I do differently?

If you want another opinion, here are three alternative, more specific questions you could ask. In *How to Lead When You're Not in Charge*, Clays Scroggins would ask these of coworkers:

1. What did I do over the past few years that inspired you?

2. What did I do that frustrated you?

3. What do I not know about myself that has become a blind spot?"[63]

People who are more reserved or shy—who are less likely to speak up in a group or even alone with you—might surprise you with their frank, written feedback. I certainly was. In April 2018, I sent an e-mail to 22 members of the senior management team I lead and asked them my three questions above. Here are some of the responses I received:

"Stay more engaged, less distracted"

"Pay more attention to detail"

"Ask harder questions"

"Ensure clarity"

"Limit emails to only most important"

"Worry less about being nice"

"Address bad behavior"

"Avoid gratuitous 'thank you's'"

"Mine for conflict"

"Lead with the 'why' more"

Ouch. My feelings were hurt. Why was that? It is because I care, I trust them, I know they care about me, and, of course, I know that there is at least some truth (if not a lot) to what they wrote. Here's another painful experience I want to share with you. I was a coach for an advanced leadership development program. So, full of pride, I offered my recent workforce communication plan I personally authored as a case study to dissect and learn from. It was the final piece of a massive workforce planning effort for hundreds of employees, and I just knew the advanced leadership development program students would validate my fine work. They would ask me questions not only about how I did it, but how I did it so well. I just knew my communications plan—if not my entire workforce plan—would become a case study. Oh, it became a case study alright. An ancient proverb says that "pride goeth before the fall."

Well, I fell alright—right into the trap of believing that because I was a good talker, that I was also an excellent communicator. I was not aware at that time of Irish playwright George Bernard Shaw's advice: "The single biggest problem in communication is the illusion that it has taken place." The group of students removed my illusion with their conclusion that not only did my plan have problems, but I was the biggest problem. They said that I needed to speak more candidly about the plan, tone down my optimism, allow more time for staff to grieve loss, and that I must address negative comments more directly.

Tony Sutherland, author of *Leader Slips*, said, "We all have the inclination at times to immediately reject criticism without taking time to process it. Yet, if we resist too quickly, we may also miss the treasure of truth that lies just beneath the surface of the criticism."[3] The treasure of truth is what you richly deserve to hear. You may learn you talk too loud, too close, too much, or that you don't talk enough, or with your mouth full. I could go on, and that's just stuff about talking. A wild approach to leadership is to intentionally hurt your own feelings. The principle way to do that is to accept that others' assessment of us is never wrong. Never? No, never.

German philosopher Friedrich Nietzsche may have taken the concept to the extreme when he said that "There are no facts, only interpretations." However, I think he was helpful when he also said: "You have your way. I have my way. As for the right way, the correct way, and the only way, it does not exist."

People are never wrong in their feedback to us. Either they are a little right, a lot right, or they perceive they are right. We can make strides from it all.

Where others are correct about a mistake we have made or a flaw we have, then fix it. Where they are not right, you have a communication issue to address. Recognize that there is almost always some amount truth to what people say—wisdom to share with you. Maybe they are 90% off base in their assessment, but that means that there's 10% to work with, to improve! There's no percentage so small that we can't take something away from another's perspective and make positive changes. In order to receive feedback, we must first ask ourselves a question. In order to build a strong foundation of character, have we, for others, made it...

SAFE TO SPEAK?

I worked on a national team of 17 executives—collectively responsible for nearly 3,000 employees—who all said that they want to hear critical feedback. Yes, all 17 out of 17 said, essentially, give it to me straight. However, exactly 0 out of 17 said they liked to give critical feedback.

Why is it that while we are hesitant to provide critical feedback at work or with our teams, we readily give it straight to our children, partners, and other close loved ones at home? It is because we feel safe to speak? Critical feedback in a safe environment is a result of strong, safe relationships. In an article called *A Culture of Candor,* the authors wrote that, "The only effective antidote (to providing candid feedback) is to create an unimpeded flow of information and an organizational climate in which no one fears the consequences of speaking up." The challenge, however, as they described it, is that "In all groups there's a powerful desire to belong. Everybody wants to be liked, to be part of the 'family'."[16] This is especially true with speaking up to top leaders. Megan Reitz and John Higgins wrote in the Harvard Business Review that, "...personal agendas play out all the time in what we choose to say to one another. This is especially the case when you occupy an influential role...Leaders often have an inflated idea of how easy it is for others to speak honestly to them. Our two-year research study, including interviews with over 60 senior executives, as well as workshops and case studies, illuminates a glaring blind spot: We simply don't appreciate how risky it can feel for others to speak up." [31]

Those we lead must know that they are safe to share frank feedback, and that we will not react to or retaliate for honest perspectives shared. We must demonstrate specific actions in the moment: not interject or get defensive.

We must create a safe environment where our team members feel we have their best interests in mind and that we want their honest feedback so we can be our best for them. This often takes years, rarely months, and never just days or weeks.

Trust is built on dependable, repeated actions more than by fleeting words. We can build a team culture of public and polite feedback. Then, as trust grows, we can push past the polite and not stop at the first response. When we hear, "oh, I don't have any real issues," respond quickly with, "but what's an example of a small thing I can work on." What is small to them will be great input for you. They may bait-and-switch and instead say, "You know, you are good at (so-and-so)." Don't take the bait. Prod less gently and say, "but what would it take to get me better or to be the best at that." Until you build trust and get good at asking for input in person, anonymous feedback—though challenging to receive also—is most helpful. It takes time to build trust. More on this topic can be found in "Where's the Beef?!" in the upcoming chapter on collaboration. Until then, let us start in the best place we can to strengthen our character and build trust, as we…

SEEK ONLY TRUTH

Scottish poet Andrew Lang warned us not to use facts and figures, "…as a drunken man uses lampposts – for support rather than for illumination." Blaise Pascal, drawing on his diverse experiences as a mathematician, physicist, inventor, and theologian, remarked that, "People almost invariably arrive at their beliefs not on the basis of proof but on the basis of what they find attractive." I often settled early in my career for partial information when deadlines were pressing, or, worse yet, when that partial information was favorable to my position. I would have been well served by the advice in *An Enemy Called Average*: "Seek not success. Instead, seek the truth, and you will find both."[52] It is both the right thing to do and the smart thing to do, especially when the stakes are high.

Getting the *right* facts and the facts *right* can be a matter of life and death.

Suppose, for example, "…that people falsely think that some risks (a nuclear power accident) are high, whereas others (a stroke) are

48

relatively low. Such misperceptions can affect policy, because governments are likely to allocate their resources in a way that fits with people's fears rather than in response to the most likely danger."[51] In *The 7 Habits of Highly Effective People*, Stephen R. Covey shared that when his daughter Jenny was only two months old and very sick, his wife called their family medical practice and reached a doctor on call who didn't know the Coveys well. The doctor answered the phone from a loud football game. Mrs. Covey described the child's condition and the doctor quickly diagnosed what he thought was the problem, and then said that he would call in a prescription. Left unsettled by the distracted response of the doctor, the Coveys wisely called back and asked the doctor if he realized their daughter was an infant. He did not. That medicine dose intended for an older child could have been fatal to the baby.[21] Let us question what we think we know. While we seek only truth, get the *right* facts, and get the facts *right*, as leaders it is indeed helpful to also…

ASSUME THE BEST INTENTIONS

Mahatma Gandhi said that the moment there is suspicion about a person's motives, everything becomes tainted. So, a wild approach to leadership is to start with an assumption that others have the best intentions. The exceptions are the pushy used car dealer, the free credit card caller, and any masked person with a weapon of any size.

We are hard-wired to *not* assume others have the best intentions. It is indeed a wild approach to think otherwise, to trust. We want information to understand our environment and make choices to ensure our safety. What I learned in my college wildlife ecology course is that our most fundamental need as humans is to be safe; we are biologically programmed to enhance our survival as a species. Our genes have been alert for 10,000 years for a saber-toothed tiger about

49

to pounce, but in the modern workplace the instinct to pounce on another person without knowing the full story has career consequences. Assuming the best intentions of others is a hard choice, but it is indeed a choice. It is indeed a career choice said Jack Greenberg, former leader of McDonalds: "I have found that the two best qualities a CEO can have are the ability to listen and to assume the best motives in others." This approach is helpful in love and life itself.

Even the most optimistic and upbeat among us conjures all sorts of bad scenarios possible in the absence of information, and we stick to our comfortable mental routines. In *Managing the Unexpected*, the authors say that "…we actively seek out evidence that confirms our expectations and avoid evidence that disconfirms them…people assume that the world today is pretty much like the world that existed at the time the (mental) routine was first learned."[56]

When we do not assume the best intentions of another it is because we lack information, and we most often misunderstand. I saw a quote on a bulletin board that said, "The worst distance between two people is misunderstanding." I disagreed with that at first. Wouldn't two people at terrible odds with one another, but who understand each other, be worse? Maybe. However, when we disagree and understand each other we have a starting point; we know where each other stands. We can then work from there to find compromise or respectfully agree to disagree. But overcoming misunderstanding first requires that we clear up misinformation and then go from there.

Everything we believe, do, and say makes sense to us—just as what others believe, do, and say makes sense to them.

When we don't understand another's beliefs, actions, or words, we make assumptions and judgements. We not only explain to ourselves what others are doing, we also act as if we know their motivations. Isn't it telling how we want to be judged by our actions, but we often judge others by their motivations? But we are quite often wrong. The sad, unfortunate thing about misunderstanding is that it is entirely avoidable. It is a gap in information that is easy to close, and the answer learned the hard way is straightforward. Are you ready for the secret?

Just ask. Just talk. When we start with what we could do better, trust and rapport grow more quickly. My son Dane, once wisely wrote (perhaps after he witnessed me again mishandle a disagreement with his mother),"own your slice—own your percent …it doesn't mean you're fully responsible, but be responsible for your percent." When we find ourselves thinking, "I don't understand why she says…" or "I don't understand why he believes…." then it's time to focus on the "I" part of the problem. Misunderstanding often results from lack of clarity around intentions. So, be clear. Literally say, "my intention is X," and, equally important, be explicit about what your intentions are not. Literally say, "My intention is not to Y." Then let us educate ourselves by asking them. Author Clay Scroggins suggests that it helps to say, "If I saw it your way, I would understand why you feel like you do and why you're doing what you're doing."[63]

A key part of "assume the best of intentions" is to avoid preconceived notions. How do we do that, though? Ask Bo because…

BO KNOWS

How do I know Bo knows? He showed me in his driveway.

Bo Diddley, a rock and roll pioneer and hall of fame inductee, rose to stardom in the 1950s. He re-emerged in the limelight three decades later through Nike's "Bo knows…" commercial featured alongside another Bo—football and baseball legend Bo Jackson. Bo Diddley, like Bo Jackson, was described as having larger-than-life abilities and personality. That's how I imagined him. That is, until we met.

The saying "do not judge a book by its cover" dates back to at least the mid-19th century, appearing in the June 5, 1867, edition of the newspaper, the *The Piqua Democrat*: "Don't judge a book by its cover, see a man by his cloth, as there is often a good deal of solid worth and superior skill underneath." Almost a century later in the 1962 hit song, *"You Can't Judge a Book by the Cover,"* Bo Diddley, further popularized the phrase. I met Bo Diddley by way of his grandson, Garry Mitchell, my friend and high school basketball teammate. I picked up Garry at his house when the "Bo Knows" commercials were still airing. Bo came out to see us. He was in good health but walked slowly down the unsteady steps of his double-wide mobile home, across the driveway from Garry's mom's mobile home. Bo had an old rag in one hand and a spray bottle of engine cleaner in another. He shuffled over to my old car, kindly nodded his head, and said only, "Let me show you something." He then cleaned my car engine. That was it. It was kind, helpful, and simple. It was not a rock and roll show, but it did rock my world. Bo reminded me that perception and reality can be worlds apart. He who once could afford servants and a mansion, could live happily in a humble abode and serve others.

A basic leadership principle is to not judge a book by its cover, but a wild approach to leadership is to actually open the book and read a few pages.

Despite my lesson from Bo, I continued to judge people and once I literally judged an actual book by its actual cover. I was searching for a bedtime story to read my youngest child, Matthew, when I saw *He Bear, She Bear* on the shelf. By its title and cover image, I jumped to the conclusion that this book would foster old gender stereotypes that I did not want to pass on to my son. On the inside cover I noted that it was written nearly half a century ago, in 1974, and that further raised my suspicions of outdated ideals. Those ideals were confirmed—or so I thought—in the first six pages. First there was the image of the mother bear in a house dress, and then there was the daughter bear with ribbons in her hair. When the matriarch proclaimed, "I'm a mother. I'm she. A mother's something you could be," I was about to close the book—once and for all. Then something caught my eye. She Bear turned to her brother, He Bear, and exclaimed "But there are other things to be. Come on, He Bear." She Bear then confidently took the lead, and over the next 28 pages we learned how She Bear (and He Bear, too, to be fair) could be a doctor, build a house, bulldoze roads, or serve as a police officer.[4]

I judged people by appearances too often. It saddens me to think who suffered at my unfairness, what friendships had I missed, and all the opportunities I lost to learn from others. Now, I try to give a book—and people—more than a few pages. Speaking of books and judging by perceived appearances, after a bedside prayer and before a forehead kiss, I would whisper in my infant daughter Taylor's ear: "you are powerful, and you are loved." I continued this little ritual for a more than a decade before I checked in with her just before her teen years. I stopped this time to ask instead: "Taylor, do you know you are loved?" She enthusiastically nodded her head. I then asked if she knew she was powerful. She shrugged her shoulders, unsure. Terribly bothered by that, I told her that I just read a book about leadership called *Lean In* by the Chief Operating Officer of Facebook. I asked my daughter what she thought the Facebook leader's face might look like. She thought for just a moment and offered: "Chubby with a beard?" I asked why she assumed it was a man. She shrugged like before. Mad at the world I exclaimed, "Facebook's leader is a woman!" I then followed with an unsolicited, passionate lecture about how Taylor is powerful and capable of anything she sets her heart and mind to, whether she leads a small team or runs a giant company one day.

Leaving Taylor's room, the usual short walk back down the hallway seemed longer than before. How might I do better? How might we all? Well, one way is to not stand still, frozen in time, while the world moves on. We must...

"PUMP YOUR ARMS!"

My old high school cross-country coach had a wild approach to our grueling 3-mile race through forest and fields. One August afternoon, with temperatures in the upper 90s in the Florida sand hills, my coach yelled: "Viker! Pump your arms uphill! Uphill is where you gain the most ground!" As I dug the front half of my running shoes into the sliding sand, I thought he was crazy. "...and make it even harder in the hardest part of the course?!" I thought. Three months later, in the inaugural year of our high school's cross-country program (which included me and another 8th-grader because our high school was too small to find enough runners), our coach led us to a third-place finish in our district and then a respectable eleventh place in the state of Florida.

Other coaches taught their runners to take it easy uphill but seize on downhill momentum to gain ground on an opponent. Our coach taught the opposite. He said there was a psychological advantage to his way: work hardest when things hurt the most. Make your opponent think you had more in the energy tank and that an attempt to pass would be futile.

Fast forward three decades...I found myself in another three-mile race. It was fundraiser event that I did not train a long time for, but I still wanted to do my best. A much younger man closed the gap between us until he was at my heels until the last big hill. At the foot of the incline, words from three decades prior washed over me. The ghost of my old cross-country coach yelled, "Pump your arms uphill!" A few minutes later, and just a few feet past the finish line, I bent over, sucked whatever wind I could pull in, and pressed the heel of my hands just above my knees. Barely able to speak, I told my younger opponent, "hey, great race." He replied, "When I saw you pump your arms on that last big hill, I knew I couldn't catch you at the end, so I didn't try." I was out of breath while he was less winded. He could have beaten me, but he didn't *think* he could.

It is the same in life as in a race. When things are most challenging, step up the pace—this trains our minds to take on and conquer other challenges.

We naturally gravitate toward a path of least resistance. A safe approach is to act boldest when things are going well—when our course is obstacle free, energy tanks full, resources flush, and time is not an issue. A smooth downhill coast makes us think we made the most progress, and we may have up until that point. But what about when times get tough? Try the wild approach. Pump your arms. Though we *may* gain ground in a practical sense, we *will* also reveal in those times of adversity our true character in full. We will discover just how powerful we are in our own right and increase our influence as a leader. General Douglas MacArthur was asked why he remained in dangerous circumstances instead of seeking cover. The General replied: "If I do it, the colonels will do it. If the colonels do it, the captains will do it, and so on."

I figuratively fell one holiday when I had a chance instead to make great strides, but I now give thanks for that. It was literally…

THANKSGIVING

I will never forget where I stood, what was said, and how I froze and compromised my integrity, cold turkey. It was mid-afternoon on Thanksgiving. Though I was to the right of the back door on the patio, I stood on the wrong side of who I wanted to be.

A relative of mine told a story that mocked the accents, height, and faces of a group of Latino men. I went from understandably shocked to unacceptably frozen. I was locked in some combination of being unprepared, unwilling, or afraid to respond. My actions, or, in this case, lack of action, was not coherent with my belief that all people have equal, inherent value and beauty. Tish Harrison Warren said in *Liturgy of the Ordinary*, "…my habits reveal and shape what I love and what I value, whether I care to admit it or not."[68].

My inaction that Thanksgiving festered in me like an internal wound until I could right a similar wrong. It was one year later to the day, same holiday, different relative, but a similar character challenge. A derogatory comment was made about another minority group. This time I spoke out and it caused some strife. Though that relationship was impacted for a while, I strengthened my integrity and increased my positive influence on others. I now give thanks for those two Thanksgivings.

More powerful than a defense of strangers is to honor colleagues and friends who are not there to defend themselves.

We earn loyalty with those present by loyalty to those absent.

The author of *Speed of Trust* wrote: "By behaving in ways that build trust with one, you build trust with many…people who talk about others behind their backs often seem to think that it will build some kind of camaraderie and trust with those who are there. But that exact opposite is true…they think you'll do the same to them when they're not there."[45] We must not only be, but we must also do. What did Mahatma Gandhi, Jesus of Nazareth, Martin Luther King, Jr., Mother Teresa, and Nelson Mandela all have in common? It was not skin color, culture, religion, or a unique period of time they shared in history. It was strong character. It was a consistency of their beliefs and their actions.

As we conclude this chapter on character, think of an acquaintance or someone famous who had some sort of advantage by violating the law, rules, or common decency. Did they get caught in the long run? They may win the battle, but they lose the war; they think they gain the world, but they lose their soul. It is a daily struggle for all of us to strengthen character and align beliefs with our words and actions. In that daily struggle, we must build good habits. Frank Outlaw, president of BI-LO Stores, said we must put our character into actions: "Watch your thoughts, they become words; watch your words, they become actions; watch your actions, they become habits; watch your habits, they become character; watch your character, for it becomes your destiny."

This chapter ends with a timeless quote about character by President Thomas Jefferson. It is advice that guides me when most other instruction fails: "In matters of style, swim with the current. In matters of principle, stand like a rock." As leaders we must be a rock others can depend on, as the essential key to...

CHAPTER 3

$\bullet - \bullet$

Collaboration – Unite Our Teams

INTRODUCTION

E ffective collaboration can literally be a matter of life and death. Go on YouTube and search for people dropping coffins. Do it. A compelling case is made, with no need for words, about the critical nature of collaboration. Two can't pull in different directions; one side can't lift while the other rests. You might say effective collaboration extends its essentialness to the afterlife. But first, let us focus on the here and now.

This chapter on collaboration follows those on connection and character for a reason. Others will not collaborate well with us until there is mutual trust.". The authors of *Helping* write that, "Teamwork and team building are increasingly seen as crucial to organizational performance, whether we are talking about a business, and athletic competition, a family, or just two workers coordinating their efforts. More books are written about team building than any other aspect of organizational development"[20]. However, a key component of fostering collaboration—not covered sufficiently in articles and books—is the power of admitting mistakes and learning from failure.

What is enabled through strong character, builds connections, and enhances collaborations.

A wild approach to leadership is to publicly and regularly celebrate failure in our organizations.

Except when dropping coffins, we must be okay to fail within our teams.

Intelligent failure is a thoughtful plan with good intentions that did not go as anticipated, but it enables us to learn. Teams and individuals must be officially permitted to lose or to fail intelligently. To be clear, fail *with* a purpose, not fail *on* purpose. Let us create a culture that shares and learns from failure. To foster collaboration and ingenuity, intelligent failure should be appropriately recognized, including through awards and other incentives. This is a difficult concept to embrace, as it is counterintuitive and popular culture suggests that failure is bad. In our win-obsessed world, mistakes are rarely admitted and many are covered up, impacting creativity and collaboration. Given that, let us consult four of the brightest minds of the last 150 years to guide us. Automotive pioneer Henry Ford said that, "A setback is the opportunity to begin again more intelligently." Ichiro Honda, building on Henry Ford's success in the automotive industry, said, "To me success can only be achieved through repeated failure and introspection. In fact, success represents the one percent of your work that results from the ninety-nine percent called failure." Albert Einstein said, "I think and I think for months and years. Ninety-nine times the conclusion is false. The hundredth time I am right." Thomas Edison took failure to orders of magnitude greater than Einstein, saying with good humor, "I have not failed. I've just found 10,000 ways that won't work."

As this intro suggestions, this chapter on collaboration—how we work well with others—has a significant focus on learning from mistakes. That is where my best learning is found. I have unintentionally created a lot of material over the years to share with you now. So, let's get started. Current and future leaders, know the following: crazy as it may sound, if you...

SCREW UP, RESPECT GOES UP

A wild approach to leadership is to embrace the counterintuitive reality that others will respect you more after you make a mistake. Your humanity grows, along with others' trust in you—provided you admit your mistake, apologize, and not repeat that same one for some time. The concept of Screw Up and Respect Goes Up runs counter to what was once taught about leadership. However, a flurry of recent thought argues in its favor. Tony Sutherland writes in *Leader Slips* that "Failure is actually necessary in order for us to become ... authentic and relatable leaders...by hiding our failures, we actually rob people from the needed inspiration for true growth."[3] John P. Kotter writes in *Sense of Urgency*: "To be human is to mess up; to connect you must fess up. That's how you maintain your integrity and regain your credibility."[40] In *5 Gears* the authors say that "Influence rises when people admit their mistakes, unless of course they make the same mistake consistently...people respect people who admit their mistake and then hustle to do better next time."[54]

Here's a quote from me for you: If you screw up, you'll still move up, if you fess up and make up. I know that sounds more like Dr. Seuss than doctor-authors I quote above, but at least it's memorable. Most importantly, it's true.

People know we are human and want us to acknowledge our humanity. They know they mess up, know that we do too, and need to talk about it all.

The Marlboro Man, however, did not. The Marlboro Man advertising campaign that ran for many years was clever, but the Man himself was not. He was ignorant about the fatal effects of cigarette smoking and oblivious to the life-altering effects of equating strength with rugged independence (Hey, I'm trying to make a leadership point, so just go with me here). Imagine what would happen if the Man got lost on his way and fell off his high horse into a rocky crevice. Imagine that there was no way he could get out without a helping hand. Is asking for help in this situation a weakness? No, he would immediately become stronger with a third and fourth hand pulling him up and out of his tight spot. The weakness was not in the Man's request for help, but in some combination of factors that may or may not be within his control: an improperly marked trail, a poor decision, or faulty eyesight.

What tight spot are you in right now financially, medically, or in relationship with others? Are you stronger going it alone? Pride is the weakness; asking for help is a strength. Ancient literature advises us to remove the plank in our own eye before we point out the speck in another's eye. Perhaps we can acknowledge our 20%, 30%, or 40% responsibility for a problem, even if we believe the other person is "more wrong." We may find that by opening up and acknowledging our flaws, especially first, the tone of the conversation completely changes, and the other person will more readily admit their mistakes. This works well in the workplace and certainly in personal relationships.

A wild approach to leadership is to regularly and publicly admit that we need help. In fact, let us say what's true of all of us: we need a lot of help, and we need it every day. Popular culture teaches that asking for help is a weakness; that one should be strong enough to do it alone. However, asking for help gives you four hands instead of two and two minds instead of one. Let us now take this concept one step further and experience even more powerful results. We not only admit the individual mistakes we make and ask for help, but also...

PUBLICLY ACKNOWLEDGE YOU SUCK

If you are willing, you can take an even wilder approach to leadership: regularly and publicly acknowledge that you suck. Admit your many weaknesses; call them out in public. Point out that your eraser gets worn down long before the other end of your pencil does.

In a cleverly titled section called, "Display Your Own Incompetence," the authors of *The Practice of Adaptive Leadership* said to foster a culture of learning, experiment with displaying your own incompetence...inspire (your team) to adopt the same level of openness and courage..."[22] What will often happen is captured by Steven M.R. Covey in *The Speed of Trust*: "When a leader says, 'I could have done that better—and I should have!' it encourages others to respond, 'Well, no, I was really the one who should have noticed that. I could have supported you more."[47]

Acknowledging your overall weakness—as opposed to just individual mistakes—carries greater emotional risk, but can reap tremendous rewards for improving organizational transparency, trust, and effectiveness. This concept is among the wilder approaches in this book, so I go to greater lengths to cite others. Know however, that there's a great deal of agreement in leadership author circles. John C. Maxwell wrote in *The 360 Degree Leader*, "People who are real, who are genuine concerning their weaknesses as well as their strengths, draw others to them. They engender trust. They are approachable. And they are a breath of fresh air in an environment where others are scrambling to reach the top by trying to look good."[50] The authors of *Measure What*

Matters say: "Transparency is scary. Admitting your failures—visibly, publicly—can be terrifying."[67]

This may be among the hardest concepts to embrace and implement, but can I share something else with you?

Everyone knows our weaknesses already; there will be no surprises to them. The surprise will be ours when a culture of trust grows with our transparency.

Five-time college basketball national champion coach, Mike Krzyzewski, said, "When a leader takes responsibility for his own actions and mistakes, he not only sets a good example, he shows a healthy respect for people on his team." There is no better way to show that respect than at home. It wasn't until more than 20 years into my marriage that I followed the advice of the authors of *5 Gears* who also said, "when your spouse says something hard to hear but is true—be quick with: 'You are right; I do that often. Will you forgive me'?"[54] There has never—not once—been a time in my marriage that I regretted opening a conversation about my weaknesses or failures, but there are dozens (my wife might say hundreds) of times I led with how I was right and then regretted it. If there's any consolation, consider the Nobel Prize-winning psychologist who said he, "genuinely enjoys discovering that he was wrong, because it means he is now less wrong than before."[74]

So, I'd suggest that to better collaborate at home and work, we private and publicly acknowledge we suck. Then we listen carefully to the responses and reactions from others. One caveat, however: keep in mind that...

NO ONE TELLS IT LIKE IT IS

No one tells it like it is. People only tell it as they see it; they share *their* perspectives and feelings, but almost never a universal truth.

Let's say that we agree that Bobbi is holding a rock, but we will not agree just how heavy the rock is, its exact color shade, how rough it is, its shape, if it's odorless, if it looks nice, if it's useful—and on and on.

How we see things is filtered by our unique nature and nurture—our one-of-a-kind physical sight as well as our unique psychological spin—from our genes at birth and what we experience in our jeans each day.

Clay Scroggins writes: "How we see the world has less to do with the way the world is and more to do with the way we are."[63] Roderick Kramer takes it a step further in *Rethinking Trust,* writing that we see what we want to see, and that "...we pay attention to, and overweight in importance, evidence supporting our hypotheses about the world, downplaying or discounting discrepancies or evidence to the contrary." Kramer went on to write that this "confirmation bias"—seeing what we want to see—would not be so unproductive if we were not already, "...heavily influenced by the social stereotypes that most of us carry around in our heads. These stereotypes reflect (often false) beliefs that correlate observable cues (facial characteristics, age, gender, race, and so on.")[15]. The authors of *Switch* added another factor for us to consider. They wrote that in, "...this entire book, you might not find a single statement that is so rigorously supported by empirical research as this one: You are doing things because you see your peers do them."

Therefore—and this is a big therefore as in therefore we must do something about it—as leaders we must always be mindful that our lens and the lenses of those around us will be as diverse as we are numerous. Do you want ten unique perspectives on an issue, idea, or opportunity? Talk for more than a few minutes with *any* ten people in the world.

A wild approach to leadership is to ask others what they feel like when they follow us. Our vantage point is full of biases and self-fulfilling prophesies and is a *dis*advantage point if not considered alongside the perspectives of others. We must ask for feedback on things we need to work on to strengthen our collaboration with others. Sometimes you'll hear what you'd expect, and other times you will think to yourself...

ARE WE ON THE SAME PLANET?

The fog lifted on Fontana Lake after dawn to reveal the second tallest mountain range in the eastern United States. I was in a wild training course that took me by boat deep into the Great Smoky Mountains. We were far from civilization. The boat captain pointed to a rustic cabin tucked into a cove and explained that it was used in the 1994 movie *Nell*, starring Liam Nelson and Jodie Foster. Foster played a wild child who raised herself unaware of the modern world. My fellow students and I, on this cool summer mountain morning, envisioned a celebratory day on this final session of the year-long leadership training program. By late afternoon, however, with the air humid and temperatures soaring to the upper 80s, most were hardly in the mood to celebrate. At one point we believed we had reached the end of the hunt, yet another clue was revealed. The instructions led us to the rocky shore of an island then up an even rockier, steep incline. We slipped and sweat as we scrambled over rocks, and I scraped my arm on thorns. It was close to dinner time; surely the final treasure would be revealed atop this hill? Alas, the clue said we were on the exact opposite end of the island from where we needed to be. Later, back at the boat ramp parking lot and finally done for the day, we compared notes. Depending upon who you asked, one would have thought it was either a treasure hunt or wild goose chase. For some it was fun, while others it was frustrating. One of our older class members, nearly in tears, described the whole affair as "cruel." In contrast, our youngest member, described the day-long exercise as "whimsical." Were we not in the same boat on the same lake doing the exact same exercise? Yes, but how they perceived and enjoyed the day (or not) related to a great many factors, including their age, personality, physical fitness level, and their unique experience that day. The list goes on, and the combinations are infinite. In *Think Again*, author Adam Grant wrote that some participants of a psychological experiment developed for World War II spies said they felt "anger, chagrin, and discomfort. However, others in the same experiment called the experience "highly agreeable" and even "fun."[74]

I once arrived in Washington with a bang. I walked straight into a glass wall on my way to the first day meetings. The 30 or so people I was about to meet with were on the other side of the glass. I also arrived a few minutes late, so I worked my way to the last chair left in the corner of this packed room. Halfway there I stumbled as my rolling suitcase got caught on someone's chair, the zipper finally gave out, and the suitcase unpacked itself onto the floor. The national chief of my organization, chuckled and said, "Well, David, you might as well introduce yourself to those who don't already know you." A mostly uninhibited extrovert with a flair for the dramatic now and again, I seized the moment for an off-the-cuff introduction. A friend and colleague who I later learned was my complete opposite—courtesy the DiSC personality instrument we completed as a group— described my entry and introduction as awkward and disorganized...so *he* thought. How could he? It was whimsical. It was free-wheeling and fun...or so *I* thought. And so goes our meetings, lives, and leadership.

Would you say there's nothing typical or predictable about your work, team, and family meetings or gatherings? If we are to collaborate effectively, we must remember that (a) we all bring a different perspective into conversations, and (b) we all leave a conversation with a different experience, having heard different things. Sometimes we see as well as hear different things. We wonder sometimes, are we the same species? Are we on the same planet? The answer, fortunately, is yes and yes.

Our individual differences when harnessed are our collective strength.

It's just a matter of how to harness that strength. The best way to *start* is to respect differences and acknowledge unique needs. Though well-intended, the Golden Rule is a self-focused approach that assumes another's needs are like ours. Let us think better and bigger, because that little nugget is...

FOOL'S GOLD

A wild approach to leadership is to break the Golden Rule. The phrase "Do unto others as you would have them do unto you" is well-known and often repeated. However, the so-called Golden Rule is more like Fool's Gold, the nickname for the mineral iron pyrite that has tricked us for centuries. It resembles real gold, but iron pyrite, a prevalent sulfide, is also used to produce sulfuric acid. So, there you have it. Fool's Gold is common, superficial, and ultimately creates something that can burn us.

Treating everyone as we want to be treated is equivalent to the poor advice to "treat everyone the same." To better collaborate one-on-one or in groups we must instead treat people as unique individuals. We all have innate wiring or traits developed through time that result in unique perspectives, needs, triggers, and motivators. Even Henry Ford, the guy who gained fame by mass producing identical cars, said, "If there is any great secret of success in life, it lies in the ability to put yourself in the other person's place and to see things from his point of view—as well as your own."

So, instead of the Golden Rule, let us follow...

The Diamond Rule: Let us treat others as they want us to treat them.

    We are all, at bare minimum, diamonds in the rough, but diamonds nonetheless. The diamond-person may ask us to help them polish or smoothen the rough edges, and we can do so but according to their unique, individual needs.

    When we see others as at least diamonds in the rough we not only consider their potential as people, but it may help when we need to extend some grace. This approach is especially useful when a rude driver cuts us off in traffic, the fast-food drive-thru window person forgets the fries with our sandwich, or the unaware guy cheering and shuffling down a packed aisle at a ballgame spills his drink on us. How I deal with those situations may sound silly or simple, but it works for me every time. What I do is this: I take a deep breath and say to myself, "This is a precious diamond in the rough made by our Creator." I find myself then more forgiving in that moment, reminded how I too make frequent mistakes and can be forgiven.

    We *can* choose to believe the best in others. That is, provide the most generous explanation for another's behavior. Leaders especially must remember that as we climb an organizational ladder, we can lose our perspective of what it was like back on the ground. Researchers wrote in the *Harvard Business Review* that, "Being genuinely curious about other perspectives requires a humility that can be in short supply...as you head up the organizational hierarchy."[31]. Other research has shown that the most successful relationships (notably, marriages) are ones in which each person chooses to believe the best in the other. We can apply that to work colleagues and strangers as well. Maybe that rude driver who cut you off in traffic rushed to the hospital to arrive before his daughter was born. Perhaps the guy who spilled his drink on your lap at the ballgame didn't realize he did it. Maybe the drive-thru window person forgot your fries because it was their first day on the job. Those are stories I told myself. Two real stories follow.

Dr. Steven Covey shared a personal story in *The 7 Habits of Highly Effective People* about when he became increasingly agitated at a father not controlling his sons' wild behavior on a train. When Covey confronted the man about their behaviors, the father non-defensively and sadly agreed. Then he added that the boys don't know what to do with themselves, having just come from their mother's funeral.[21] How's that for a shift in perspective! In an instant, Covey went from wanting to condemn the man to wanting to help him, now having profound sympathy.

Tony was a great salesman, which meant he was constantly on his phone. Each night he paced the baseball sidelines at practice and sometimes even games. The way he waved his hands and was so expressive with his face, I figured he was trying to convince someone of something. So, while he made money and probably lots of it, I and other parents volunteered to coach his son and other kids.

I later learned however that Tony was a pastor, paid poorly, and each night helped others through depression, debt, divorce, drugs, and death. To this day, Tony is one of my mentors and dearest friends, and is the author of *Leader Slips*. I could provide lots of material if he decides to write a sequel! When we learn to see others from their point of view, we can grow from a foolish Fool's Gold perspective, advance past the Golden Rule, and ultimately elevate our leadership to view others as the diamonds they are or can be.

We are designed for relationships; we are meant to support one another. It makes life easier and more fun. We all need a hand from time to time because sometimes we are all...

DANGLING FROM A HOOK

Let us never underestimate the generational impact we have—
what long-term events may be set into motion—by those we lift
up…or those we take down.

Dangling from a locker room hook on a wall, with legs flailing
above the floor, was a 5'6" teenager, abandoned there because of his
big mouth. My 6'5" father reached up, unhooked and lowered him,
and said (as I imagine it in his thick New York accent), "Ayyy, yo, my
name's Aw-knee (Arne). Whatch-yawz?" In a timid whisper the
response was, "Kenny." The two became best friends. They were one-
part 1908 cartoon Mutt and Jeff—one tall, one short, and always in
trouble—and the other part 1958 real-life Zuko and Kenickie from
Grease. Arne and Kenny wore faded blue jeans, rolled cigarette packs
in their white tee shirt sleeves, and slicked their hair back with engine
oil. These youthful collaborators had too much time on their hands
and extra room in the trunk of Kenny's car. The car trunk was a great
place to hide for the "four-for-the-price-of-two" drive-in movies. That
trunk was where my dad became acquainted with Kenny's sister, my
mother. We just never know what hangs in the balance when we lend
a hand to another.

Though not as spacious as the back trunk, under the front
hood of Kenny's car was ample space for a wooden crate to hold many
spare parts. These extra parts were not for Kenny's car, though. They
were a random assortment of parts from other cars that Kenny and
Arne thought others could spare, though they never bothered to ask
the owners. Kept under the hood, these parts were not for show. They
were for *the* show. Not the drive-in picture show, but the live-action
drama that unfolded at the first stoplight an agitated motorist honked
their horn, thinking Arne and Kenny took too long to get it in gear.
Their horn would trigger Kenny's horn (by way of a homemade switch

71

under the dash) to blare nonstop. The homemade switch next to that one caused black smoke to billow from under the hood. The show began in earnest when Kenny would pound the steering wheel in an exaggerated mock frustration, while Arne would, in feigned exasperation, step out of the car, look at the car behind them with his long arms extended and shoulders shrugged. The waiting car behind them—the one who honked because the pair was taking too long—could not see the exact details of the melodramatic tinkering under the hood that followed to "repair" the alleged problem. However, what was visible was car parts flying out from under the hood, over their shoulders, (pulled from the box of collected, spare parts), now scattered around the intersection. Just when the smoke supply stopped, and long after the building line of car drivers' patience were exhausted, another switch was flipped to silence the blaring horn. That development triggered Greaser handshakes, for then it was time to get the broom and dustpan out of the trunk and sweep up the parts strewn about the intersection. All the while, the traffic light turned red and then green and then red again. My dad said that one time, unbeknownst to them, a policeman watched the whole thing, too overcome with laughter (and perhaps admiration) to bring a legal case against them. The case had already been made: never underestimate the power of creative collaboration, believe the best in others…and don't honk your horn too quickly!

Let's step back from these stories and consider that, like my Uncle Kenny, we all dangle at times on this large ball that turns and sails through the universe. A wild approach to leadership is to remember that in almost every situation we could benefit from another pair of arms to lift us up, or to help us firmly plant our feet on the ground. To collaborate well one-on-one we must be there for one another to help respond to tough times. There is absolutely no hard stop between our "work lives" and "our personal" lives. We all just have "lives"—and just one life in fact—so we all need each other. We need each other to solve problems. However, to lead our teams well, we must anticipate challenges and involve others in decisions. This is how we put...

COLLABORATION IN ACTION

The Senegalese have a proverb: "If you want to cut a man's hair, it is better if he is in the room." If you had the same reaction that I did, we have some questions for the Senegalese. Perhaps then let us not think too deeply on that proverb other than to glean that to get better *buy in*, it helps to *be in*. Collaboration can be a messy, inefficient endeavor. General Stanley McChrystal writes: "Getting to know your colleagues intimately and acquiring a whole-system overview are big time sinks; the sharing of responsibilities generates redundancy. But this overlap and redundancy—these inefficiencies—are precisely what imbues teams with high-level adaptability and efficacy. Great teams are less like 'awesome machines' than 'awesome organisms.'"[17]

To foster great collaboration of an awesome organism, after we gather others, we must empower them. John P. Kotter, Harvard University professor and leadership author writes in *Leading Change*: "Without sufficient empowerment, critical information about quality sits unused in workers' minds and energy to implement change lies dormant." Kotter said that methods to increase empowerment include, "...flatter hierarchies, less bureaucracy, and greater willingness to take risks...senior managers focus on leadership and in which they delegate most managerial responsibilities to lower levels."[55] The more collaborative option of engaging others does not result in loss of authority, however. Leaders still make decisions—and can always have the final say—but we do so after we bring our team deeper into the ownership process. We want them to see projects as theirs—empowered to make ideas happen and see them through to completion.

If an issue is either simple, not very important, or there is not much time, a decision by a leader without gathering much input makes most sense. However, if an issue is either complex, critical, or time allows, deep engagement by others will always lead to a better decision. There are many options to gather input. A "collaboration continuum" I developed through years of doing it the wrong way has helped me at work, coaching sports, and at home. To put collaboration into action, we strive for the engage or delegate end of the spectrum rather than simply just inform or consult.

Inform – let others know what you're doing and don't ask for input
Consult – ask for input and adjust based on others' feedback
Involve – engage others at key points to help develop the decision
Engage – work closely with others throughout the whole process
Delegate – turn the decision process entirely over to others

To put collaboration into action, also consider that valuable information—or perhaps even the silver bullet solution—can come from any member of the team. That is, if we take the time to listen. A great idea can come from someone we normally do not trust or someone we don't even like. One of the many benefits of keeping an open mind and an open dialogue—including with those we normally disagree with—is that one great idea among many bad ones, or one simple solution that you needed, can emerge. What follows is an extreme and very personal example.

In the Cajun bayous of south Louisiana, where the passing of time could be mired in the swamps, three older coworkers couldn't conceive how at 23 years of age I would still be unmarried. So, Don Brevelle, Brent Bordelon, and Dexter Soileau, took turns finding me a mate for life in a story akin to Goldilocks and the three bears. Just mere months removed from the University of Florida, where more than 35,000 students provided ample dating opportunities, I had little faith and little interest in the Cajun trio's small-town endeavor. Don Brevelle and his wife arranged for a double date with a lady who was much too old for me. Next, Dexter Soileau set me up with a candidate who was several years too young. So then, I resisted a third attempt by Brent Bordelon. Hearing of Don's and Dexter's failures, Brent's research revealed that my blind date was my exact same age—born just 15 days after me. However, he also told me that her nickname was "Lulie," allegedly bestowed upon her by her senile great-grandmother. Her legal middle name, "Cotton," was her dad's nickname, bestowed upon him after a bad bout with blonding bleach. Given that information, I was concerned about blind date number three. However, Brent did say that our meeting would be to *laissez les bon temps rouler* (let the good times roll) by way of an informal backyard group event with unlimited boiled crawfish, corn, and potatoes—my new favorite meal. That last piece of information was helpful data that swayed my decision. Now, more than a quarter-century later and a half century old, I think back to that blind date and our *cochon de lait* (pig roast) second date, I'm quite grateful for Brent and my Cajun wife, Lulie.

I took a chance at collaboration in action. I didn't need a panel of experts with diverse, well-framed opinions to advise me. In *Think Again*, Adam Grant writes that while, "…knowledge is best sought from experts, creativity and wisdom can come from anywhere."[74]. I just needed to keep an open mind that the best opportunity may come from a most unlikely source. I thought of the African proverb in considering the Cajun feast: "Examine what is said and not who speaks." Effective collaboration can be quite the unifying affair, especially with the help of boiled crawfish or a roasted pig. Other times, we must pause and ask…

WHERE'S THE BEEF?!

Two days after I got my driver's license in 10th grade, I was hired at Wendy's fast-food restaurant at $3.45 per hour. They needed help on the heels of their wildly popular television campaign featuring the elderly curmudgeon woman with a culinary ax to grind. She would exclaim at the counter of a fast-food rival: "Where's the Beef?!"

Though I didn't bring home much bacon, I learned soon enough where the beef was at Wendy's. After I mastered french fries, I spent many a long, hot day with spatula in hand beside the grill. Next up was kitchen cleanup. To this very day, I ask that you don't mess with my kitchen; there is too much pride at stake and nostalgia in play. My children have many times heard that I am, in fact, an award-winning kitchen cleaner. I have the certificate to prove it. In August 1987 I was Employee of the Month for my sparkling fast-food kitchen. I received a wall plaque that graced my garage wall for years. New responsibilities followed me to front register and then the pinnacle of fast food: drive-thru register. After 18 months I went from $3.45 per hour to $3.75 per hour. I certainly didn't run the place, but I knew Wendy's well. It was hard to leave, but when Walmart offers you $4.00 per hour, you can't look back. One thing I did reflect on years later was a priceless lesson in hard-wiring collaboration.

We won't review quarterly earnings of Wendy's or Walmart in this section, nor will we read a pithy quote from either company's past or present chief executive officer. Instead, we will simply draw on my real-life, entry-level experience at these corporate goliaths. I learned a lot back then about "us versus them" and "subteam pride." The Walmart where I worked intentionally varied work schedules so there was no "us versus them." In contrast, Wendy's had a set of employees for the day shift, another group that worked nights, and third bunch who worked mostly Saturdays and Sundays. Like the competing cattle farmers and sheep farmers in the old American west, where the phrase "I have a beef with you," originated, there was strife between the separate shifts. It was warring tribes at worst and players in the blame game at best. "Where's the beef?!" Oh, there was a beef to be had for sure when one group of employees arrived to find the buns not stocked, the kitchen a mess, and the salad bar critically short of croutons. More than just the negative impact on employee morale, there was lost productivity during shift transitions. No one had incentive to leave the place better than they found it. Why fix someone else's mistake with whom you had no allegiance? Let the next group literally clean up the mess. At that one restaurant at least, that approach affected Wendy's bottom line. Leadership expert Andy Stanley shared in a 2018 podcast that many people come to work thinking about themselves first and their team or department second, leaving the overall organization in third place. Stanley said it takes intentional connecting of the dots or collaboration at the top to dissolve silos.

What I experienced as a young Walmart employee was that we won't have to dissolve silos that aren't there to begin with. An employee's shifts were intentionally varied. Two of the employees to arrive as I clocked out might include the lady and gentleman who I might work alongside the next day, and one of them and someone new might work with me the day after that. Two days later, all of us might work side-by-side. There could be no "them" in that shift work scenario. However, within a work shift and a workforce overall, we do want healthy "subteam" pride, a delicate consideration that a team leader must manage. A team is strong when their subcomponents are strong, so long as the sub-efforts add to and do not detract from the larger organization.

The success of an organization depends upon the ability and willingness of a subteam to subordinate their goals to the broader team mission.

Team is a relative term, though, and almost every team has one or more subteams. Subteams are essential for effective function of the larger team. The 11 players on a football field include lineman and backs, the 9 on a baseball field include infielders and outfielders, and even the 5 on a basketball court include guards and forwards. In the workplace the combinations are endless: engineers, sales, budget and administration, maintenance, executives, and the list goes on. The football running back would be tossed to the ground if the five football lineman did not close ranks. The basketball forward would not score if the guards' dribbling and passing did not synergize when faced with a full-court press. Subteams are by design, necessary as a component of division of labor. We need the engineers' collaboration to ensure safety and efficiency, we want the sales force to share contact lists to match potential clients, and we must have clear communication between maintenance staff to trouble-shoot and fix problems. General Stanley McChrystal described the need for cross-team relationship in his book *Team of Teams* when he wrote, "We didn't need every member...to know everyone else; we just needed everyone to know *someone* on every team, so that they thought about, or had to work with, the unit that bunked next door...they envisioned a friendly face rather than a competitive rival."[17]

When a leader needs help to unite seemingly disparate groups, take a wild approach: signal SOS. No, not the international code of extreme distress, but what I call the internal SOS or "Strategic Overlap of Staff" to improve communication, foster efficiencies, and solicit new, synergistic ideas. SOS strategies can be very simple. You can add to this list below; it's just a start. Some are pragmatic, and some are symbolic:

→ mix up work shifts rather than have set people on set hours to maximize new contacts.

→ host all-staff meetings monthly or quarterly and not just gather within communities.

→ have one larger, central break room rather than smaller ones scattered in departments.

→ develop new employee orientation with more overall mission and less technical focus.

→ appoint teams, committees, and work groups that include all work disciplines.

→ in weekly or monthly newsletters spotlight employees over time from all work disciplines.

→ ensure that you and other leaders spend one-on-one time and group time with all.

Greater collaboration takes a short-term time loss in efficiency for a long-term time gain in effectiveness. So, with respect to *horizontal* integration, let's have strategic overlap. But with respect to *vertical* authority, let's just ...

TURN IT UPSIDE DOWN

A wild approach to leadership is to turn our entire team upside down. We do this two ways: literally with our organizational charts and figuratively with our philosophy.

Every organizational or "org" chart I've seen shows the big boss on top—the power at the pinnacle—and who reports to who in the supervisory chain as it cascades down from the top boss. Org charts look like a pyramid with the boss at the point, and, as it gets wider at the bottom, the front-line workers. Whether a team of four people or a corporation of 4,000, all org charts I've seen look like a pyramid. Is there another way? Yes. Turn that piece of paper 180 degrees to the left or right. Turn it upside down. Given that organizations have the most impact—have the most people and touch the most product—at the widest point of that pyramid, why not show the front-line workers at the top? Then we show the boss at the bottom as the foundation of support—a servant-leader who others figuratively and literally (on the org chart) grow outward and upward from. When we explain this new org chart to our teams, we emphasize that leadership exists to serve the team and not the other way around. So,

79

that's the piece of paper and the symbolism. How do we put that philosophy into action? At least weekly—if not several times per week—ask your team members who report directly to you on the org chart, "what can I do to help you today?" Then actually help them. Expect them to say and do the same for their direct reports. This will serve as a clear test of who wants to lead for their sake or for the sake of helping others. The author of *Hand Me Another Brick* warns us that, "Being a leader is an unenviable calling. It appears glamorous and glorious to the novice, but it is more often lonely and thankless...the best leaders are actually servants."[38].

> The greatest mark of leadership is advancement past the role of hero to that of another's guide.

The authors of *The Starfish and the Spider: The Unstoppable Power of Leaderless Organizations* wrote that, "We look for hierarchy all around us. Whether we're looking at a Fortunate 500 company, an army, or a community, our natural reaction is to ask, 'Who's in Charge?'"[57] Past history and popular culture often teach that the role of leader is best executed as the devil's advocate, hard-liner, referee, or cop. So when we turn that approach upside down and focus less on who's in charge and more on the leader as the "cheerleader, coach, facilitator, and nurturer"[49], we can transform the ownership of an organization or team. Dr. John Maxwell suggests in *The 360 Degree Leader*: "Instead of trying to be Mr. Answerman or Ms. Fix-it, when your leaders start coming into their own, move more into the background. Try taking on the role of wise counselor and chief encourager."[50].

Donald Miller says that what, "is true in business, in politics, and even in your own family. People are looking for a guide to help them, not another hero."[12] Leaders no doubt lead, but that is often best done in service to others. When I hear a supervisor mention an employee and say that he or she "works for me," I can't help but think that supervisor may be some combination of socially unaware, a micromanager, or arrogant. I'm sometimes wrong, but too often right. Instead, if we hear an employee of ours say within earshot that they work *for* us, I suggest we gently interject with something like, "we work *together for*" (our organization). John Wooden, widely considered one the greatest college basketball coaches in history, won 10 national championships. Hundreds of young men looked up to him and hoped through his leadership that they might go from unpaid college student to rich, professional basketball player. Wooden held their future in his hands and a whistle tightly clenched between his teeth. Wooden became a widely sought leadership guru, and once said simply, "Make sure that team members know they are working *with* you, not for you." If he can, we can. I have defended the need for top-down, chain-of-command structures in certain areas or organizations like factory floors and the military, but even in those institutions change is underway. General Stanley McChrystal, a veteran leader of modern warfare who recognized the need for change to advance efforts in the Middle East, wrote in *Team of Teams*: "Increasing complexity of the world...requires greater adaptability, and adaptability is more characteristic of small interactive teams than large top-down hierarchies... This new approach also requires changing the traditional conception of leader. The role of the leader becomes creating a broader environment instead of command-and-control micromanaging."[75]

Centralized organizations—especially those with a single, strong leader—may be easier to weaken. Weaken the leader and weaken the entire organization. Whereas in decentralized organizations, powerful teams rise up and see themselves as the responsible party. The word *responsible* can be broken into *response* and *able*. Responsible people are empowered people who are able to respond. They see things as their problem or their opportunity instead of waiting for someone else to address the need. Responsible people are more likely to take the steps needed, and they do so with the ideas from many minds and not just the leader's. This is how the internet grew. This is how large-scale change often happens. In 2018, young people, numbering in the hundreds of thousands, saw themselves as able to respond and walked out of their high school classes at the exact same time all across the United States—in small towns, suburbs, and city schools alike—to protest gun violence in schools. There was no single clear leader.

Let us dispense with the old chain-of-command, top-down strategies that were necessary to win old wars and stay safe in aging factories. Let's symbolically show through the upside-down organizational chart our advances in these modern times. While we're at it, let's get wilder still. Let us have a ...

COLLABORATION DEBATE

I lifted my head off of my pillow, looked away from the television for a moment or two, looked back, and slowly shook my head. Clenching my eyes closed, I thought that there must be a better way.

I just witnessed one of the worst moments from one of the most divisive presidential debates in modern history. I laid awake in bed staring at the ceiling fan before a wild approach to leadership came to me: what if we flipped the format and made the candidates have a collaboration debate? An oxymoron you say. How can one collaborate and at the same time debate? What if for just one in the series of televised debates, the format was on areas and issues of agreement between the candidates? Instead of arguing about disagreements, they must provide explanations and ideas on how they would collaborate to implement an idea or project. Let's step this down to the United States Congress. What if the House of Representatives or Senate members had to spend the opening days of each session with an identification of two or three areas of common ground? What if within those proposed bills or existing laws, they fine-tune and update language, and all the while build relationships and restore trust? The hope being that each side of the aisle realize, "that wasn't so bad," with the primary goal being the epiphany that "*they're* not so bad." With that as foundation, they can move forward better equipped to address areas of less agreement. General Stanley McChrystal was able to successfully bring disparate, secretive groups together within the military and intelligence agencies. He said that "The critical first step was to share our own information widely and be generous with our own people and resources. From there, we hoped that the human relationships we built through that generosity would carry the day."[17] General McChrystal's efforts completely changed the United States' military approach in the middle east and then reversed its fortunes. If the military can do it, why can't Congress and the President? Well, let's not get ahead of ourselves. How about we start within our span of control, a little closer to home on Main Street, on our street, or around our dinner table. It all starts with us, and the logical first step is in our own homes, neighborhoods, and at work. Therapist Michelle Kinder wrote: "...practicing social and emotional health in our own homes, even in small ways, can lay the groundwork for a return to civility and connection."[25]

In our collaborations, should we settle for, "I get 50% of what I want, and you get 50% of what you want?" That's not collaboration. Nor is collaboration, "I can live with getting 40% of what I want this time and you get 60%, but next time we agree to 60-40 my way." That is compromise.

Collaboration occurs when we commit to rich discussion and robust debate in pursuit of a common goal. The result is often that we create something entirely different and better together.

Stephen R. Covey uses the word synergy to describe what happens in effective collaboration. He said synergy results in a whole greater than the sum of its parts. Synergy, "...creates new untapped alternatives; it values and exploits the mental, emotional, and psychological differences between people." His son, Stephen M.R. Covey, warned us against "scarcity thinking." In his book, *The 3rd Alternative*, the younger Covey tells us not to get trapped, thinking that, "there's only so much pie on the table, and if you get more, I get less…the polite outcome of scarcity thinking." Like his father he inspires us to, "adopt the abundance mind-set that there are infinite, rewarding, exciting, creative alternatives we haven't even thought of yet."[47]

An analogy I like to think of is that I'm the knee, you're the hip, and Gertrude over there is the ankle. Individually we can all bend to some degree, but when we collaborate together, we can jump a hurdle, sprint past the competition, and complete a marathon. Before we run off too far with that analogy, we must first ensure that collaboration can be sustained. That is only possible with early, often, and excellent …

CHAPTER 4

Communication — Tell The Story

INTRODUCTION

If there is one thing I have screwed up most in my career and in my life is this: I thought I communicated something, but I didn't. This chapter is worth the read if only to improve our personal relationships, but the Harvard Business Review said this about our careers: "The number one criteria for advancement and promotion for professionals is an ability to communicate effectively."

Three decades into my career and more than a quarter century in my marriage, my greatest struggle remains how to effectively communicate what's most important. Even for those of you who are very good at communication, it is the one box we can never check as complete. I have erroneously led myself to believe that because I'm an energetic extrovert who talks a lot—and with a lot of people—that I am communicating what's most important. More challenging still is when I share a lot of information before and after my main point, and then the key message is lost. Journalist Sydney J. Harris said not to confuse information with communication: "...Information is giving out; communication is getting through."

In the academic world some add unnecessary words to papers to either impress or to meet a minimum word requirement. Outside of classroom walls we must speak even more plainly and simply to effectively communicate. To lead successfully we must follow the advice of General Colin Powell: "Great leaders are almost always great simplifiers, who can cut through argument, debate and doubt, to offer a solution everybody can understand."

In the 21st century, information is instant, comes at us many ways, and is massive in amount. Therefore, it is critical that we are compelling, clear, and concise when we communicate.

That takes a lot of work, but it's not complicated. Writer Earl Wilson said: "Science may never come up with a better communication system than the coffee break." Though we often need to communicate in a variety of ways, it is often best done one-on-one. The reason this chapter on communication follows Connection and Collaboration chapters is that only half of communication is saying or writing words. The critical first half is listening. The Latin origin of the word communication is to *share*. That is, you say something, and I say something about a topic, and we increase our shared understanding of it and one another. We keep in mind all the while that a dialogue never consists of two monologues. Before we cover many "do's," let's open with what we should…

NEVER, NEVER, NEVER

It is widely believed that Winston Churchill's shortest speech on record was when he stood up at a college commencement to deliver only these words: "Never, never, never give up!" Then he sat back down. The truth is that never happened. Many things never did happen that are reported as true. The internet and social media reach far and travel fast, so it's important that we do our homework. The

Washington Post did theirs in 2012 and learned that Churchill gave a fine speech that had a theme of "Nevers" in it, but it wasn't those exact words and certainly wasn't that brief. As we start our communication journey, let us start with getting our facts right and not make assumptions. Therefore, I offer the following "Nevers" for your consideration:

- Never assume the older lady is his mother...
- Never suggest he stand up...
- Never assume she's pregnant...
- Never say there's something on his tooth...

... because that may be his wife, he may be unable to walk, she may have just gained some belly fat, and that dark spot may be where there is no tooth. I actually avoided all four of these near-misses somehow. On the first one, the words were literally coming out of my mouth: "Oh, this must be your..." before the gent interjected, "...my wife." I still shudder three decades later when I think of that. As cringeworthy as that was, it can be worse, with more serious relationship implications.

I asked a friend from more than two decades ago how his nephew was doing. This friend of mine was not married and did not have children. His nephew was like a son to him, and he like a second father to his nephew. In hindsight, I did recall him telling me a few years ago what happened, but I must not have listened carefully enough to commit the event to memory. After a pause, he reminded me that his nephew, his pride and joy, died in a traffic accident a couple year prior. I should have remembered that.

The very first section and story of this book, You Must Have Two Mouths, emphasized the importance of listening. That is by design, just as the introduction of this chapter suggests fewer words. So let us minimize the use of our one mouth and maximize the abilities of our two ears. Take the words of Abraham Lincoln, a quote rooted in wisdom from literature thousands of years ago. It remains timeless: "It is better to remain silent and be thought a fool than open your mouth and remove all doubt." Booya! Take that! Booya? Yes...

BOOYA!

When we have listened carefully, and it is indeed time to speak up, we may have trouble getting our point across. Is your quiet voice not heard at the break room lunch table? Do you feel marginalized around your own kitchen table? I have a suggestion. It's called "booya," and I learned this wild approach from one of my wild relatives.

There is some debate about the origin of the word booya, but one thing is clear: it must be said with vim and vigor. We pronounce it as follows: "BOO-yaaaaa!" A booming first syllable that is crisply separated from a fading second syllable. We must all say BOO the same, just with different volumes and our ya can be yaaa, yaaaaaaa, or yaaaaaaaaaa, depending upon how we are feeling at the moment. No one says booya better than my cousin Billy. Billy Nicholson defies convention and embodies booya. He has a wild approach to getting his point across. It's a little easier for him than most, to be fair. Billy is a lovable, loud, uninhibited extrovert from New York, and he has a very strong accent. To make sure he is heard, Billy waits for the right moment and verbally explodes with infectious enthusiasm.

I've tried to booya in meetings, and it works almost every time. Rather than float your small wave of an idea known amid a raucous sea of brainstorming, wait until the calm after the storm. When the room is silent, even for just a brief moment, unsettle the peace when you say your piece. Say it loud and say it proud just like Billy did at a packed baseball stadium in Atlanta, Georgia.

Billy was anything but a face in the 40,000-person crowd when his New York Mets came to town to face my Atlanta Braves. Family is family, but baseball is baseball, so we made no effort to buy tickets together. We sat far apart, about one-third of the horseshoe-shaped stadium across from each other.

Large crowd dynamics are unpredictable, with a stadium almost deathly quiet for random periods of time. Acoustics can be stranger still, especially in the old Turner Field, a stadium built for the 1996 Olympics but insufficiently retrofitted for baseball. Billy seized the crowd dynamics and harnessed the acoustics. When the stadium was briefly silent, he bellowed as if through a bullhorn: "VIE-cuhhh! VIE-cuhhh! VIE-cuhhh! BOO-yaaaaa!" I spotted him a hundred yards away as he again hollered my last name, Viker, in his thick New York accent: "VIE-cuhhh! BOO-yaaaaa! "

The still-quiet stadium turned to watch and listen. Billy was working his way down his aisle as he bellowed. Everyone was cheering him on. You see, people everywhere loved Billy's infectious enthusiasm. From afar I saw three ushers descend towards him but quicker than you could whistle, "Yankee Doodle Went To Town," the trio was laughing along with Billy, shaking his hand, patting his back, and playfully ushering him back to his seat. "BOO-yaaaaa!" Billy got me. To this day, I don't remember who won the game, but I do have this story.

Until I did some research, I thought Billy made up the word booya. I know he helped spread its use, maybe more than anyone else along the eastern seaboard. Billy used it with explosive excess at even the most seemingly insignificant of times. When Billy found what he was looking for on grocery store aisle four, he yelled "booya!" even if he was all alone, and he said it no quieter than the loudspeaker lady saying, "cleanup on aisle three." If on first try Billy pumped exactly $20.00 of gas with no additional clicks needed, it was "booya!" If he inspected his just-sharpened number two pencil and it had a sufficient point: "booya!"

I recommend a hearty booya approach to life at large, but if that's too much for you, let's land this plane where we first took off:

> When something matters deeply, share it with an emphatic, impactful, "BOO-yaaa!"

A booya will ensure you are heard, and others will know that you mean what you say. Let's make believe we're in an important meeting right now. No whispering. Think about what you want to add to the discussion, and imagine yourself delivering your point clear, concise, and compelling, as if you were saying booya. Let's practice together. Say it loud and proud. "Booya!" Again. "Booya!" Again. "Booya!!!"

I think you get the point. Enthusiasm is contagious. Now let's focus on when we need to...

ANNOY YOURSELF

A wild approach to leadership is to say something until you are annoyed with the sound of your own voice.

When people don't do as we ask, it's not always because they are insubordinate. People don't follow our instructions for a variety of other reasons: they were not paying attention, they could not hear us, they didn't understand what we said, they started thinking about the first thing we said and missed the second thing, their mind drifted off to what they wanted to say, or they just saw a squirrel out the window and forgot all else in the world. My youngest, Matthew, couldn't wait to come home and recite the Pledge of Allegiance he learned in preschool. His chest swelled and face beamed towards the end: "...with liberty and just as frog."

My experience has shown that there is about a one-third chance our message was heard, understood, and also remembered. Throughout this book we dismantle many old adages, but we also expound on several truisms that are as helpful as ever. Here's one: tell them what you're going to tell them, tell them, and then tell them what you told them. Teachers, preachers, and motivational speakers will even say things three times in a row. Surely you have noticed that car commercials and other advertisements will repeat the same phrases over and over—and over and over. It annoys us, but we remember it. My oldest son, Dane, said that his strategy to deal with his father's poor memory was to think of a thrown rock skipping across a lake: the first few times it bounces off, but eventually it sinks in. Several years before that, Dane, then a teen, applied this principle unknowingly. He was concerned that his youngest sibling Matthew, a four-year-old picky eater, was not eating enough protein. Dane made it a daily grind to lecture the stubborn younger one about the importance of eating meat. Dane told Matthew time and again how much he would love steak when he grew up. This went on for months. It annoyed us all. About the time I wondered if Dane's message to Matthew would ever sink in, I asked Matthew about what he wanted to be when he grew up. He responded quickly with one authentic, run-on sentence: "when I grow up I'm going to marry momma and steak is going to be my favorite food."

General Stanley McChrystal shared his repetitive communication approach. He wrote: "I tried to remember 'less is more,' and stick to a few key themes. Experience had taught me that nothing was heard until it had been said several times. Only when I heard my own words echoed or paraphrased back to me by subordinates as essential 'truths' did I know they had been fully received."[17] Even when we think people may not consciously listen to us, their subconscious might be.

For most of the nearly 20 seasons I coached youth baseball I was the third base coach. My main job was to give instruction and encouragement to the players before they even stepped into the batter's box. This was no small task because a small person would soon have a very hard ball careening toward them on an unpredictable path. There was no way for the batter to blend into the crowd like a pile of football players. In the batter's box, standing at the plate, it is you against the world. Everyone, including those in the stands, are watching. I recalled the advice of legendary college basketball coach John Wooden who said that "It's not what you teach, it's what you emphasize" that matters. After years of trial-and-error, I developed a number of little phrases that I would repeat time and time again. These might not make sense to you, especially if you have never played baseball, but to former players of mine, who might read this book years later, they would know just what to do when they heard: "Protect the plate," "Tough with two," "3 and 2 is the same as 0 and 2," and "Yes, yes, yes!" Maybe they are using these phrases now with their own children in a backyard Wiffleball game. That would make me smile. The phrases I used were memorable not because they rhymed or were cleverly worded. They were memorable because they were repeated over and over—and over and over—and over again. I knew they would start sinking in with the players about the time each year that I would become annoyed by the sound of my own voice, and when the players would mockingly say them to one another in the dugout. I did not get mad when I heard the phrases used derisively; I was pleased they were now part of the team vocabulary. Among the treasures in my attic is a quilt parents gave me at the end of one season that had the phrases stitched all over it.

The timeless advice of "tell them what you're going to tell them, tell them, and then tell them what you told them" is equally applicable for a college paper, when we speak to a large audience, or when we have a crucial conversation with a friend. President Abraham

Lincoln took it a step further. He would write a letter to his generals, tuck the letter in his coat pocket, then summon them to the capitol or visit them near the battlefield. After the conversations, Lincoln would hand them the letter to keep and then say something like, "this is what we just talked about." The generals could then refer back to the letter when they did not recall exactly what was said during—or expected after—their conversation with the president. Great Britain's Winston Churchill emphasized this approach the next century: "If you have an important point to make, don't try to be subtle or clever. Use a pile driver. Hit the point once. Then come back and hit it again. Then hit it a third time – a tremendous whack."

Communication gets trickier the more people we involve because we all hear and process things differently. So it is critical that to get our message across to a diverse audience, we must say things many different ways and many different times. How many times? "When you are tired of saying it, people are starting to hear it," said Jeff Weiner, the CEO of LinkedIn. This approach can have an exponential effect on an organization. This trickle-down effect of a leader repeatedly emphasizing things will multiply up and down an organization. So, annoy yourself with the sound of your own voice. Annoy others too, but make sure it doesn't come to a…

BAR FIGHT

So this guy walked into a bar…

He ordered a drink and stood between the TV and the table where my oldest son, Dane, and I sat to watch the 2019 National Basketball Association finals. What I *should* have done was walk up to the man and politely asked him to move over just a little.

What I did instead was solicited input from a group of people standing next to our table, asking them if this guy was in their way too. Their ringleader, very drunk and very loud, informed me that, no, he was not in their way, and that the man in question was her husband. The woman then badgered us while we sat quietly at our table, as if we were the loud ones blocking the TV. Hearing the ruckus, the husband turned to my son and asked why he was harassing his wife. I am not sure if it was Dane's emotional maturity or his 6'3" muscular frame that settled the man down. However, for one of the longer minutes of my life, I feared my son would get punched and a bar fight would ensue.

The incident was avoidable—and what I wanted achievable—had I spoken *directly* and politely to the gentleman.

As I think back to uncomfortable encounters at work or when I coached youth sports, how many would have been handled more successfully had I dealt directly and politely with the other person? What I had done too often in the past was delay the uncomfortable, got frustrated, and then, clouded with unhealthy emotion, handled things poorly.

There is often a better communication alternative than the one we choose. The author of *The 3rd Alternative* said that "The best leaders don't deny or repress conflict...They know there is no growth, no discovery, no innovation—and indeed no peace—unless the provocative questions are brought out into the open and dealt with honestly."[47] I have advised my children and shared with my work colleagues the oft-repeated phrase, "It's not just *what* you say it's *how* you say it." But let us remember that the reverse of that is just as relevant: "It's not just *how* you say it, it is *what* you say." So, what do you say we agree right now, to improve our communication, we say *what* is the matter, and say it directly and kindly? Perhaps we'll avoid a bar fight, and, depending upon how that goes, there is a chance we may have to...

"PUT 'EM UP!"

I first met Bubber (yes, that's his name, not Bubba) when he threw the handcuffs on me. He was a respected instructor at the Federal Law Enforcement Training Center, the place I, and the other students, had gathered to learn case law, how to shoot guns, wield batons, and use pepper stray, among other things. Bubber was teaching us new game wardens how to handcuff the bad guys and gals. Besides his unique name, there was something else that made him very different: his thick Mississippi accent. More than just Bubber's word pronunciation was his use of a word or phrase that would completely confuse us non-southerners. Bubber ended day one of our training with the following instruction: "awl-riiiight y'all, PUT UP yer handcuffs." Southerners dutifully bent over and placed them in their equipment bags, knowing exactly what the man meant. Meanwhile, the rest of the class—those from the West, Midwest, and the North—all quickly raised our handcuffs up in the air as if clamoring to ask a question. How could two very different actions result from a seemingly simple instruction?

In Bubber's part of the country I learned about a judge who called for a recess during a hearing for a minor incident, which became a major one after some miscommunication. The judge looked at his timepiece (watch), grabbed his billfold (wallet), and said it was time to break until after dinner. The defendant from Pennsylvania, not knowing the exact hour but afraid to ask the judge for clarification, made sure he was back before "dinner" time, the last meal of the day. Little did he know that in the rural south, "dinner" was lunch, and "supper" was dinner. And so when he returned on the early side at 5:30 p.m., he faced the wrath of the judge who had been waiting for him for four hours!

Misunderstanding can have more serious consequences than that. Edgard H. Schein writes in *Helping*: "When the cultural rules are ambiguous or misunderstood, tragic consequences occur, as when white South African managers in the gold mines punished workers for being insubordinate and untrustworthy because they were 'shifty-eyed' and 'never looked you in the eye.' What the managers did not understand was that under the tribal rules with which the workers grew up, it was a cardinal rule to not look directly into the eyes of a superior because it was a clear act of disrespect."[20] There can be fatal consequences as well. If a police officer shouts, "Hands up, now!" and a person who speaks another language thinks the order is to set down what is in their hands, the results could be lethal.

Supreme Court Justice Brandeis noted, with relevance outside the legal arena: "Nine-tenths of the serious controversies that arise in life result from misunderstanding, from one man not knowing the facts which seem important, or otherwise failing to appreciate his point of view."

It is essential—and sometimes a matter of life and death—to understand the impact of our words, especially in light of the culture we are in.

We must also not be so flippant and unaware as to just tell anyone to...

"HAVE A NICE LIFE!"

When my oldest son, Dane, was very young, he once fished quietly with his grandfather. Dane, apparently after much thought, randomly broke the silence and innocently offered: "PawPaw, you must be a good kisser..." PawPaw, looked at him confused, and waited for more. Dane explained: "...because you've been married three times." After a good laugh, PawPaw cast his line again, and likely thought no more about it. For the rest of us—until we reach the status of fishing buddies—we had best put more thought into our words.

96

Let us use great care in what we say and what we write until we establish rapport and build trust.

I knew a leader, John, who was a master at "hello," but would botch "goodbye." He did not have fishing buddy time to build rapport with everyone, so there was phrase John used that caught some people off guard. After small talk with waiters, hotel clerks, cashiers, and taxi drivers, John would end with, "Have a good life!" Unfortunately, to many Americans that sounds a lot like the sarcastic phrase "Have a nice life"—the functional equivalent of "take a hike!" Though John would say "Have a good life" with utmost sincerity and good intentions, he hadn't established enough rapport and there was hardly time to build trust. Judging by body language and awkward, unsettled responses, his well-wishes were not always received as intended. Worse still, John wrote "Have a good life" in the subject line of an e-mail following the word "Farewell" when he announced his retirement. For those who didn't know him well and chose to not read the very thoughtful and articulate email that followed, they were left to assume that he just raised his middle finger to the world in a bitter departure. Some were left with that impression, their only impression from the communication.

Since we only have so much time to reach the status of fishing buddies—and can't make people read the rest of our story or listen past our first few words—let us get to the main point quickly and chose great care with words. In the true stories above we touched on being kind in Bar Fight, being clear in "Put Em Up!", and being careful in "Have a Nice Life!" In addition to being kind, clear, and careful, we must be...

COMPELLING AND CONCISE

In a packed, loud gym with the game on the line, nine nervous and easily distracted pre-teens looked at me for the solution. This was not a time to ask for input, think out loud, and offer options. This was a time to firmly speak and quickly act.

"Okay, Asher, when the referee hands you the ball, fake a bounce pass to Alec, then hit Gideon in stride. Gideon, you streak down the right side for a layup, but if you are cut off, swing the ball to Dane for a jump shot. Everyone, get your hands in here. Together now: '1-2-3, Team!'"

Every day and all over the world, the impact of communication can be much more serious than that. Police, firefighters, military commanders, and the person next to the factory machine that can cut off a hand will all agree that information shared concisely saves lives. It hits close to home, too. Let's say your grandmother is transfixed by her new cell phone. As she saunters down the driveway, she flips between news feeds, a text from your sister, and a new picture on Facebook. Grandma does not realize she stepped into the street. A car is coming. Here's something you should *not* try at home: "Oh, hey Grandma, I have a thought. But first, I apologize for the interruption…" No, you'd yell, "STOP!" or "CAR!"

The same principle applies when we speak with groups of people. I have read that public speaking is one of American's greatest fears, more than slithering snakes or flying in a plane. One of the reasons is we feel like we must sound like a television or movie star. We don't. Whether we address a gathering of half a dozen people or a crowd of hundreds, our fear, more than of snakes, should be that we sound too much like a snake-oil salesman from yesteryear, rather than a relatable, real person right in front of them. We will be compelling not with what words we choose but how we say them with passion and authenticity. Sincerity is more effective than a pleasing voice or clever phrasing. Jules Rose of Sloans' Supermarkets said that "The exact words that you use are far less important than the energy, intensity, and conviction with which you use them."[39] That's the compelling part. The concise aspect of our public speaking will come with preparation and practice. The more we say, the more they have to remember, so let us remember Lincoln's advice to tell them what you're going to tell them, tell them, then tell them what you told them—but do so briefly.

Abraham Lincoln's Gettysburg Address may be the most famous speech in history. He said only 275 words. The person who spoke before Lincoln was paid to deliver a speech that rambled on for more than an hour. You've probably never heard of it.

The authors of *Building A Story Brand* said that "...the human brain, no matter what region of the world it comes from, is drawn to clarity and away from confusion."[12]. We must be concise. Depending upon the audience, the event, and our style, we have options for delivery: talk off-the-cuff, memorize an outline so we don't miss key themes, use talking points or slides to prompt us, or deliver a written speech. Though my favorite is off-the-cuff when I know a topic well that I am passionate about, I won't hesitate to stick to a script when the cameras are rolling, or the stakes are high. Three more pieces of advice I learned the hard way:

(1) *know our audience* – bright lights on stage once kept me from seeing who my audience was; only half of them were who I thought they'd be.

(2) *connect with our audience* – be relatable, including use of self-deprecating humor.

(3) *allow time for questions when you can* – it is more important to hear from them.

A wild approach to leadership is to intentionally unlearn what school taught us about communication. In middle school, high school, and college we learned to add extra, unnecessary words to meet the required 500 word minimum on our essays. Some would answer questions in class, trying to sound intelligent, or attempt to convince the professor that we read the book assigned by going on about anything and everything we remember about it. However, in the real worlds of our offices, court rooms, operating rooms, ballfields and battlefields, brevity is essential and its absence sometimes fatal. In this chapter about communication—in which we've covered the need to be kind, clear, careful, compelling, and concise, let's also be sure we are not...

THE HOMEWRECKER?

We were still on Cloud 9 after our Caribbean honeymoon, flying high even after landing at the New Orleans airport. Reality came crashing down, though, when we opened our front door. Someone ransacked our house. Cushions were torn, magazines ripped and scattered, and lamps knocked over. Even the loaf of bread in the pantry had tear marks. It must have been her ex-boyfriend. He was so jealous and cruel to sue to get back the big TV and the small dog right before Christmas and our wedding, so surely, he took further revenge. We called the police. After photos were taken and the officer made notes, we went to bed. We woke up the next day, however, still in the nightmare. The house was trashed again. Did the ex-boyfriend sneak in a second time during the night?

The same loaf of bread had more tear marks, and it looked like some had been eaten. We called the same policeman back, but this time to help hunt down the culprit I was certain was still in the house. I used my federal game warden skills and crept through the kitchen towards the pantry. I swiftly pointed my semiautomatic handgun, pulled the trigger, and missed. The clean bullet hole was visible in the pantry wall as my ears rung from the blast. Meanwhile, while the culprit cowered just inches away, the small-town cop, with his revolver already unholstered and ready, nailed the bad guy first try. He then exclaimed in his thick Cajun accent. "Meh, I hunted wit a fed befo', but I don dink I evuh squirrel hunted with one in his house until dis day!"

It is essential to have the facts right and not jump to conclusions when we consume information. It is equally important to make sure we send the correct information—and to the right people.

I spent the night once at my female boss's house, and her husband wasn't there. Before *you* jump to conclusions, know that my immediate supervisor, a man, was there too, along with nine or ten other people he supervised. The big boss was generous to host us all at her lake house, a relaxed, informal setting to plan for the future at work. I, however, was anything but relaxed just minutes into the next morning. The first thing I did when I woke up, even before using the bathroom and brushing my teeth, was text the following to my wife: "Good morning my precious love." The problem was, I sent it by accident to my female boss, a top federal executive who oversaw me, more than a thousand other employees, and administered the Endangered Species Act. I thought in my initial moments of panic that I'd be endangered by the boss or made extinct by my wife. I stood alone in my horror, while male colleagues woke up around me on couches and cots to the sound of a scream from the other side of the house. The scream then turned to a cackle, then devious laughter, then booming voice wrapped in a smile upon entering the room: "David, I didn't know you cared!" I was relieved beyond belief but embarrassed beyond consoling for some time. To this day, I'm reminded of that morning by colleagues who gave me the nickname "Precious."

Since that last incident, before I press send on a text message or email, I check to see that the recipient is correct, as I know that each communication is precious. I also try to check my facts better, still feeling a little squirrely from the ex-boyfriend incident. As embarrassing as it is to tell those stories, it is for the greater good. It also helps for leaders to...

BE SEE-THROUGH

A wild approach to leadership is to be *see through* in two different senses of the words: let us allow others to see through to our heart and let us be transparent in communications. The two concepts are linked. The heart comes first.

John C. Maxwell, author of *Everyone Communicates Few Connect,* said that people may *hear* our words, but they *feel* our attitude. Cold facts rarely connect with people. Maxwell cites therapist and leadership expert Rabbi Edwin H. Friedman who said that "The colossal misunderstanding of our time is the assumption that insight will work with people. The Rabbi also said, "good communication does not depend on syntax, or eloquence, or rhetoric, or articulation, but on the emotional context in which the message is being heard." Connect with the heart and the head will follow. It's irrefutable. Maxwell wrote in another of his books, *The 21 Irrefutable Laws of Leadership,* that, "You can't move people to action unless you first move them with emotion. The heart comes before the head."[46]

Given the essential nature of this topic let us hear from a few more leaders. In *The Heart of Change,* John Kotter and Dan Cohen write that in most change situations, managers initially focus on strategy, structure, culture, or systems, which leads them to miss the most important issue: behavior change happens by speaking to people's feelings.[36] Andy Stanley wrote in *Visioneering* that, "A clear explanation of the problem engages the mind...But a compelling reason will engage the heart."[37] When President Franklin D. Roosevelt addressed the nation at the depth of the Great Depression he famously said: "all we have to fear is fear itself." This was a simple recognition of people's deepest feeling. Note that he did not say, "if you adhere to these five logical steps, you will feel safe." Instead, he addressed the heart first to build trust.

> We don't always have to get the words right. Those I lead tell me they can forgive my head—especially with this mouth of mine attached to it—if I am vulnerable and authentic and share my heart.

That didn't come naturally for me, and to this day it is still not easy. I am more comfortable as an adult to create a safe, controlled *exterior*, as I will always carry some *interior* trauma from my childhood. An insightful instructor told me once that I've shared my personal story so many times that it's become a tale without emotion or a brochure with bullet points. To lead effectively with the heart we must follow the advice in *How Well Do You Know the Story of You*. "The true story of you is the key to why you lead and informs why others are drawn to follow you." McNulty says that "Acknowledging your own missteps, struggles, and pain is necessary to acquire the emotional intelligence central to leadership effectiveness."[23] Be real, and when being the real you includes being funny—or trying to be—go with it! In *Social Intelligence and the Biology of Leadership* the authors wrote that, "A boss who is self-controlled and humorless will rarely engage those neurons in his team members, but a boss who laughs and sets and easygoing tone puts those neurons to work, triggering spontaneous laughter and knitting his team together in the process...top-performing leaders elicited laughter from their subordinates three times as often, on average, as did mid-performing leaders...In other words, laughter is serious business."[18]

Our stories and our connections need less polish and brevity, but more emotion and relatability. Before there were text messages and newspapers—and even thousands of years before hieroglyphics on cave walls—we humans communicated through the spoken word. And that communication was always more enjoyable, compelling, and memorable—thus more easily repeated—when shared in the form of a story. The authors of *Scrum* wrote that, "People think in narratives, in stories. That's how we understand the world."[30]

Jesus of Nazareth, one of history's greatest communicators, spoke often in story form so his disciples could easily remember them and later share his teachings with others. For others to feel safe with us as leaders, we need to make those stories authentic and relatable. Let's get our head out of the way—and make it personal and memorable—so others can see through to our heart.

BE SEE-THROUGH, PART II

In addition to a visible heart, our communication must be transparent in that we share as much as we can and as soon as we can share it. That is done best in person. Two of America's past presidents, from two different eras and two different political parties, used two different but effective methods. They made listeners and readers feel like they heard directly and personally from the President. For more than ten years Franklin Roosevelt led the nation during the Great Depression and World War II through his evening "fireside chat" radio broadcasts. Almost a hundred years later, tens of millions of Donald J. Trump supporters received a message directly from the President of the United States on their hand-held devices through Twitter.

In their annual State of the Union addresses, Presidents George W. Bush, Barack Obama, and Bill Clinton used a technique to make a large and complex issue more personal and relatable. As they spoke from the podium at the Capitol on a variety of topics, they would pause occasionally to introduce an invited guest, seated next to their spouse in the balcony, and then talk about something that person did, related to the topic. They literally put a personal face on an issue. We can do the same in our leadership, including the authentic use of *our* real face. Why is transparency so important?

In the absence of information, we human beings fill in the gaps with information we make up, which is usually unhelpful and often untrue.

The Dalai Lama warned us that, "A lack of transparency results in distrust and a deep sense of insecurity." Charles Swindoll added more to that concept when he wrote: "Security is undoubtedly a basic human need that cannot be ignored or minimized. People typically find it difficult to concentrate on anything, regardless how meaningful it might be, when they fear for their safety."[38]

Let us never underestimate our impact on our followers. In *Social Intelligence and the Biology of Leadership* the authors wrote that, "...certain things leaders do—specifically, exhibit empathy and become attuned to others' moods—literally affect both their own brain chemistry and that of their followers. Indeed, researchers have found that the leader-follower dynamic is not a case or two (or more) independent brains reacting consciously or unconsciously to each other. Rather, the individual minds become, in a sense, fused into a single system."[18]

Robert Sutton looked at wild species for further insight. He wrote that, "Followers devote immense energy to watching, interpreting, and worrying about even the smallest and most innocent moves their superiors make. This is something we've long known about animals...studies of baboon troops show that the typical member glances at the alpha male every 20 to 30 seconds to see what he is doing ... Further, people tend to interpret what they see the boss do in a negative light ... followers are most likely to construe it as a sign that something bad is going to happen to them ...They redirect their efforts to trying to figure out what is going on and to coping with their fear and anxiety ... as a result, performance suffers."[7].

A negative reaction to an absence of information is normal. In fact, we are engineered that way. A suspicious mind, linked to a body alert to dangers, enables us to live and pass on similar genes. We can acknowledge our wild past and our wild tendencies as a species and as an individual, but we don't have to accept that as the way we must be going forward. We can choose to do better. If we recognize that we all digest most anything in the absence of facts, we can instead feed those we lead healthy, helpful information so they don't have to make stuff up. In an article titled *Social Intelligence and the Biology of Leadership* the authors wrote: "Leading effectively is…less about mastering situations—or even mastering social skill sets—than about developing a genuine interest in and talent for fostering positive feelings in the people whose cooperation and support you need."

There are some of us who are naturally suspicious and need to see things personally to understand or believe something. James O'Toole and Warren Bennis wrote in the *Harvard Business Review* that, "A culture of candor doesn't develop on its own—the hoarding of information is far too persistent in organizations of all kinds. That said, leaders can take steps to create and nurture transparency … leaders need to be role models: They must share more information, look for counterarguments, admit their own errors, and behave as they want others to behave."[16] Therefore, it is better for us to be equally aware of pros and cons of an issue—(think of math with pluses and minus and a zero net gain)—than to go just in the negative direction, imagining a variety of scenarios that have no merit. In a *Sense of Urgency*, John P. Kotter wrote that, "Anytime that employees sense that information is being kept from them…they feel like outsiders. As a result, their morale drops."[40] We don't want our team to feel like outsiders with poor morale; we need to be all insiders with high morale. The latter is how teams move forward together faster, better. The authors of *Scrum: The Art of Doing Twice the Work in Half the Time*, said that "The greater the communication saturation—the more everyone knows everything—the faster the team."[30]

Our communication must be early, often, and iterative. We further build trust and enhance morale through effective, see-through communications. This is best defined as communication with maximum transparency and minimal delay. The *Harvard Business Review* explained research into an extreme example of reliable information's effect on people. "Air-raid sirens during the bombing of London in World War II... were so reliable...that people felt free to go about their business when the sirens were silent...(but) those that were never warned lived in a constant state of anxiety."[7] Let us share everything we can as soon as we can because transparency is not just about sharing information but doing so in a way that people can quickly and independently verify the facts.

In this chapter about communication, we have covered the need to be clear, careful, compelling, concise, correct, and most of all kind—a word I wish started with the letter *c*. I hope the stories have helped, from what to "Never, Never, Never" do to avoid a "Bar Fight!" and to know when to "Put 'Em Up!" so you can "Be See Through" in your leadership and "Have Nice Life."

In all seriousness, effective communication, this fourth chapter, comes best, literally and figuratively, after solid character, strong connections, and sound collaborations—the titles of the first three chapters. So, what do we now *C* for ourselves—(sorry, I couldn't resist)—with these traits and approaches to advance our leadership? We put them into practice with the four *Ps*: people, policy, planning, and priorities. If I could have thought of better *P* words than policy and planning, I would have, but they are concise and they do capture the need for us to make decisions happen (policy) and prepare for the future (planning). We will then wrap up with priorities to ensure we focus on a few great things rather than just many good things. And it all starts with people.

Part II:
The 4 P's

CHAPTER 5

People – Develop The Best

INTRODUCTION

If you have read this far—finished the first half of this book and now started the second half—you have invested much of your precious personal time. It is only fair then, especially as we move to focus more on the people part of leadership, that I share with you more of my personal story. I start with a single moment in time. I'll go further back in time from there, then ultimately go forward in every sense.

"Viker, let's go!" he yelled. I must not have heard him the first time as I stood behind the team bus. I was lost in thought, and lost and alone in 11th grade, despite being surrounded by half my basketball team. "Viker, let's go! Load up!" I choked on the black fumes spewing from the exhaust pipe of our team bus. But I choked hardest on the words next spoken over me that changed my life forever.

"David, you need a job where you don't have to deal with people!" said team helper-dad, John Fradello, Sr. He just witnessed me, once again, say something unkind to a teammate. I stumbled up three bus steps, eyes now watering from more than the bus fumes. I slumped down alone in my second row seat. The bus rolled on to our next game, and though I leaned the side of my head on the window, glassy eyes fixed on the passing blur of north Florida cattle ranches and pine tree

plantations, I looked inward. I was not aware of our team's destination; I only thought of mine. Am I a bad person? Do I treat people badly? Is this what Mr. Fradello thinks of me? What do others think? What do I think of me? I replayed those words. "David, you need a job where you don't have to deal with people!" Mr. Fradello wasn't defending his son after something I said. He didn't come to anyone's defense. He was just making an observation, and one that was painfully true. Some in high school try to go unnoticed, but not me. I craved attention, good or bad. High scores in basketball or high grades in math was never enough. I needed more, but I looked in places that could not fill the void.

I was born a month premature, due in part to nicotine in my tiny veins and an umbilical cord wrapped around my neck. Though scrawny and yellow jaundiced, I healed, physically, from wounds in the womb. However, emotional trauma takes longer to heal. I have learned a child of an alcoholic or the child of divorce attempt unhealthy combinations of the following: to please or impress, to strive to unite, or to resort to control. It is hard to please someone though when they are not there; I came home five days a week to an empty house—actually a single-wide mobile home. It was a two-bedroom, mostly metal house with no central air. A plastic oscillating fan and open window helped me fall asleep after dark. My mother worked the afternoon and evening shift as a prison guard to help put my brother and I through school, and she slept while I was in school. My father, a mechanic in a factory, lived 1,061 miles or 16 hours and 51 minutes away by car. It was hundreds of days in between visits. I couldn't rely back then on my only biological, older brother, Erik. One of the many secrets I kept as a child was that Erik did not live with us. The thought was that if our father found out it would somehow invalidate the court-ordered child support. Erik lived two lots down a gravel road and slept in the extra bedroom of our grandparent's mobile home. He was almost six years my senior and had his own demons to conquer. He did so with the help of a rowdy circle of older, motorcycle-rider friends. One might think that with twenty-one first cousins, Erik and I could rely on others. However, they were the offspring of nine broken marriages. My first cousins include two felons who spent multiple years in jail, a third who was murdered, a fourth who died by suicide, a fifth cousin who was married five times at last count, and several others who died way too young, including from substance abuse. When I was in first grade my best friend got hit by a car one afternoon and was dead that night. No one asked me then or ever how I was holding up. So at a very early age, I installed the veneer: hard and slick on the outside to cover the raw and fragile inside. At the age of six, my survival strategy was to please or impress, strive to unite, or resort to control. Pre-adolescence, this worked out pretty well. I was a taller than average, energetic extrovert who easily led other children. The teen years, not so much. I was a very late bloomer up against bigger kids with increasingly independent minds who saw my leadership style as aggressive, annoying, and alienating—like the kind of person who would grow up to have, "...a job where you don't have to deal with people!"

After an hour into the long basketball team bus ride and long since I first choked on the fumes and choked back tears, I no longer stared out the window. I sat up straight. Decades later I remember that next moment in 11th grade. My feelings were complex, my strategy unknown, but the words that came to me were straightforward: I am miserable, and I make other people unhappy. I have to act different and be different. I started down a new path that moment. I leaned forward and looked over the seat in front of me. Bobby Sabas, my future groomsman, was asleep. I looked to my right and thought I could start with none other than John Fradello, Sr.'s son across the aisle. Jr. saw me look towards him and said: "What the hell do you want?!"

This is going to take a while, I thought. More than three decades later, I am still working on it.

As we move forward from a stronger foundation of connection, character, collaboration, and communication, where do we go first? What is the most important work before us and our most significant, lasting legacy? It is people.

How we recruit, train, mentor, coach, and treat people—how we lead people—will define our impact on the world more than anything else we do.

General Colin Powell said: *"...Endeavors succeed or fail because of the people involved. Only by attracting the best people will you accomplish great deeds."* There's not a protocol, practice, policy, project, or program that we pour our heart into that won't change or be eliminated entirely after we're gone. In fact, some people are waiting for our departure to undo many of our efforts. Hiring people, hands-down, is the most important work of a leader not only for the future of an organization, but for the present, profit bottom-line as well. The authors of *Measure What Matters* write that, "Turnover is costly. The best turnover is internal turnover, where people are growing their careers within your enterprise rather than moving someplace else...people aren't wired to be nomads. They just need to find a place where they feel they can make a real impact."[67] Even in today's culture of career moves from one organization to another, a large component of the workforce will stay with an organization for 20, 30, and sometimes 40 or more years. The most important subset of hiring is when we hire those who will supervise, manage, or otherwise lead the rest of our teams. We must get those hires right most of all. The authors of *First, Break All the Rules* interviewed employees in 400 companies and learned that "...the manager—not pay, benefits, perks or a charismatic corporate leader—was the critical player in building a strong workplace...An employee may join a company because of its prestige and reputation, but that his relationship with his immediate manager determines how long he stays and how productive he is while he is there."[11] A Gallup organization study showed that approximately 50% of people who leave their job do so because of their bosses.[64] Famously blunt President Theodore Roosevelt said that "The best executive is the one who has sense enough to pick good (people) to do what he wants done, and self-restraint enough to keep from meddling with them while they do it."

A focus on people is limitless in impact, and that is why Part II starts with people. Let us start at the very beginning—of life—and recognize that...

LEADERS ARE NOT BORN

In the delivery room for the birth of my three children, Dane, Taylor, and Matthew, I noted that each one, without exception, made the whole affair all about them. As they cried and screamed, did they stop to ask how their mother, me, the nurses, or the doctor were feeling that day? No. All they did was fuss. Then they wanted to eat. They couldn't even lift their own heads, and certainly weren't willing or able to lift a finger to help anyone else. They weren't born leaders.

Fast forward a dozen years in Dane's life to middle school. He tried to transfer out of band class, and he appeared to be a shy follower. He never spoke up in crowds. A dozen more years later, however, and Dane had become the high school marching band drum leader, was in the Georgia Tech marching band, and taught drums to high school students. Dane later received a master's degree in leadership, speaks to hundreds of people at a time from stage, and I've been glued to the television several times to watch him speak.

When I hear someone say that so-and-so is "a born leader," it aggravates me for two reasons: (a) the thought of someone anointed with an unearned advantage, and (b) the lack of recognition of others' hard work to become the good leaders they are. Legendary football coach Vince Lombardi said that "Leaders aren't born, they are made. And they are made just like anything else—through hard work." In the well-researched *Good to Great*, Jim Collins said that "Most great leaders do not start as great leaders. They grow into great leaders."[9] One of the most unproductive and inaccurate adages is that "A leopard doesn't change its spots." Well, in nature, leopards don't once they are grown up. However, people are never all grown up. We can and do change. Nature (our genetics) in addition to nurture (our experiences) can help advance our leadership a great deal; there are some who arrive on this planet with an extra dose of good memory, gentleness, quick wit, or a rousing public speaking voice. They have more of the ingredients of good leadership than the rest of us. However, they must still work hard for many years. It's just that the rest of us have to work a little harder.

A wild approach to leadership is to search more in the middle of the crowd for potential leaders. Look more for those with their heads down—the introverted, steady types—just as often as we identify energetic extroverts on center stage for leadership positions.

A common misconception, fueled by television and film, is that energetic extroversion equals dynamic leadership. Research has shown—and *Good to Great* captured it memorably—that "the plow horse rather than the show horse had the more successful track record" in leadership abilities. I have read that roughly half of Americans are introverts. That list includes some presidents such as Thomas Jefferson, Abraham Lincoln, Woodrow Wilson, Dwight Eisenhower, John F. Kennedy, and Barack Obama. All were also excellent public speakers, perhaps some of the greatest in the world. Extroverts have not cornered the market on public speaking. Strong leaders who also happen to be introverted, are more likely to better prepare for a speech and stay on message.

So, as we hire others, especially supervisors and managers with most influence over our teams, let us remember that leaders are not born, they are made. Some take time to develop, and some are right there in front of us and we don't see it; we look for the wrong thing or too much of the same thing. Our strength as a team lies in our diversity at multiple levels. Are we best served then to consider our teams (and our nation for that matter)?...

A MELTING POT?

I grew up hearing that that the United States is a melting pot, and that people from all over the world come here and blend in together as Americans. I think it is more complicated than that; I think it's better.

Not only is the melting pot view not accurate, it can also undermine a wild approach to leadership that harnesses the power of diversity. I think of America as a whole—and I like to help develop the teams I serve with—as less of a melting pot and more like a jambalaya or gumbo. These two dishes both have visibly different but wonderfully complementary ingredients—better than a melting pot which implies uniformity through conformity.

My wife Lulie is a Cajun from south Louisiana. She makes one of the best jambalayas in America, and, without a doubt, the best gumbo in the world.

My wife makes her gumbo like we should develop our teams:
-Stay personally engaged
-Research new ideas
-Use an array of ingredients
-Select only the best ingredients
-Demonstrate a lot of patience, and
-Adapts approach with new information.

My wildlife biology classes in colleges didn't teach me those timeless leadership principles, but I did learn about the benefits of diversity. Do we want to ensure long-term viability of the critically endangered red wolf? Make sure the alpha male doesn't only mate with his sister or first cousin. Whether we restore a wild population of a species or revitalize a human organization, the same principle applies: maximize the strength of our decision or result by maximizing the diversity of people and ideas.

The more perspectives we can bring to bear when we make a decision, the stronger that decision will be. When our teams and organization look more like the increasingly diverse American people we serve, we are also better positioned to market our product or service.

Let us never stop, though, at an approach towards diversity that merely consists of how people look or where they're from. If you have attended a team building training or self-awareness training you have probably taken a personality or style assessment like Meyers-Briggs, Taylor-Johnson, StrengthsFinder, RightPath, or DISC. There you learned that our uniqueness as people goes deeper still. You will find that two people who on the surface seem very similar, can be quite different. Two young, single, city-raised people of the same gender and ethnicity—with the exact same interest in books or sports—can have completely different personality types or leadership styles. They have different preferences, see the world uniquely, and, yes, even vote differently. Let us remember that not every middle-aged Christian man with his hair parted on the side votes conservative Republican. Not every 22-year-old female from the west coast votes liberal Democrat. If you greeted me in a parking lot, you might assume I am like other 50-year-old white guys you have met. You might think, "middle class suburban accountant or insurance agent" as you also notice a vague resemblance to an older Richie Cunningham from the classic television show *Happy Days*. But happy days were not always a part of my past. If you began a dialogue with me, you would learn that three-fourths of my grandparents came to America on boats from Denmark, Norway, and England, and what little money they had was in their pocket. My mom worked as a prison guard and my dad was a mechanic. Substance abuse plagued our extended family. That's my true story. Here's another's: How fortunate for our nation that President Theodore Roosevelt did not conform to what many expected from a rich, over-40, white male in the early 1900s. His ground-breaking steps are felt more than a century later. Though born to wealth and privilege, Roosevelt famously fought against corporate monopolies. He was the first president to invite an African American to dinner at the White House. Roosevelt was an avid big game hunter who also created the first federal bird refuge and started the National Wildlife Refuge System, now the world's largest network of lands and waters dedicated to wildlife. It was "Teddy" Roosevelt whose nickname became forever associated with the stuffed children's bear after he refused to shoot a restrained bear in Louisiana.

We cannot begin to appreciate the value of different people and cultures until we first see the amazing and diverse experiences, often untapped, *within* an individual. We all have a personal and powerful story, and without a doubt it is full of unique experiences and lessons learned that we draw from and can share to benefit others. Few assembled independent, diverse thinkers better than President Abraham Lincoln. He appointed to his presidential cabinet no less than four opponents who ran against him in the 1860 election. His "team of rivals" included the Attorney General, Secretary of War, Secretary of Treasurer, and Secretary of State. Lincoln valued diversity so much that he organized his presidency around this idea and made the dignity of the individual person his cornerstone priority and his lasting legacy. What will be our legacy? Who will we hire? I have an idea, and you may be comforted that...

IT AIN'T ROCKET SCIENCE

I didn't ask Beth and Tim for permission to tell you that they had 2.6 and 2.4 college grade point averages when they were hired, so I changed their first names and won't say their last names. I will tell you, though, that after they completed a developmental program their junior and senior years in college, they both raised their grades a little and then advanced their careers a lot. With only bachelor's degrees, they led dozens of employees who attended better schools, got higher grades, and achieved master's degrees and PhDs. How was that possible? A wild approach to leadership is to recognize the following:

It ain't rocket science to select potential leaders; we just need to know what traits to consider most important. It's rarely GPA nor the name on the front of the college sweater.

There are indeed some jobs where technical expertise is indeed a matter of life and death. No aerospace engineering hiring committee conversation went like this: "Hey, for our new lead NASA engineer charged with designing our first human flight to and safe return from Mars, we will give the most weight to people skills in our selection." No, we just need them to focus on the right math for a safe landing, even if someone gets offended by their bedside manner back here on the ground. Speaking of bedside manner, I want my cardiac surgeon to be less in touch with my heart than knowing what the heck to do when she touches my heart with the scalpel she used to open my chest. The same principle applies to the software designers who enable my money to move safely from one Wells Fargo account to another. I have enough indigestion when funds move from Main Checking to Kids College Account. So, for those jobs and others like them that make up 2% percent of work in the world, we need higher grades and more and specialized education. For the 2%, let us treat it like rocket science and think in terms of "3-2-1 lift-off!" and heavily factor the following three: grade point average, universities attended, and degrees earned. But for the other 98% of jobs, certain attributes predict a great deal more success. Why did we pick Beth and Tim, and why are they successful? It's not "3-2-1" rocket science. Instead it is…

THE BIG FOUR

With no further dramatic countdown nor corny buildup, let's get right to it. Why did I select Beth and Tim? They demonstrated:

- Strong work ethic
- Good organizational skills
- Contagious passion
- Excellence with people

Over the course of my career I made many mistakes; I base this book on those lessons learned. One thing I did get right was the big four. I was barely out of college myself, in charge of student programs for my organization. Today, I still measure candidates against the big four, whether I personally select a top leader or approve an entry-level hire. I wrote the big four down *on* a piece of paper once but didn't *do* a paper on them. I certainly didn't write a book about them, but a Dr. Patrick Lencioni did with a similar formula. In *The Ideal Team Player*, Lencioni wrote that the ideal team player possesses three bedrock virtues, "humble, hungry, and smart."[58] By smart, he means a person knows how to act and what to say around other people—not so much IQ as emotional intelligence or EQ. By hungry, he means energetic and ambitious but in a good way, wanting to improve self and the organization and not just self. The most critical trait is humility, rooted in one's character. Lencioni wrote that, "Humility is the single greatest and most indispensable attribute of being a team player." General Norman Schwarzkopf said memorably: "Leadership is a potent combination of strategy and character. But if you must be without one, be without the strategy." Lencioni warned that the most dangerous combination is someone who is hungry and smart but lacks humility—lacks character. Good character remains the most important building block of a leader.

When I coached youth sports teams over the years, I picked players in dozens of drafts after tryouts. With baseball, I learned to select a sufficient number of potential pitchers and catchers for those two more difficult and key positions. However, at the first practice, I let every player try out to pitch or catch for the team. I did not want to pre-select, so I gave everyone the opportunity. Many chose not to audition, but many times I would be pleasantly surprised with the talent that would emerge. My brother is a theater professor with experience as a director dating back decades. He often manages limited budgets, a small talent pool to select from to cast a show, and the purchase rights to scripts are no small sum. Erik would never write a big check for, say, William Shakespeare's *Hamlet*, without first knowing that he has least one high-quality actor who can memorize a whole lot of lines for the lead role. Erik does not pre-select that person, rather he opens auditions broadly and welcomes an even better candidate to emerge. For my brother's plays, my youth who play ball, or leadership candidates making a play for positions in our organizations, we measure them against the big four, but not just for what they can do today. We consider their potential for the future. We lean towards…

TALENT NOT EXPERIENCE

Both curious and confused, I asked my colleague out west, "So, why didn't you pick Sarah?" It was the second time in several months that Sarah Manches applied for but was not picked to be in a leadership role over several states and several hundred employees. Sarah tried a third time when she applied in my region. She clearly had the "Big Four" from the last section. I called one of my colleagues who didn't pick her to ask why. The answer I got: "Our panel thought she was not long enough in the tooth."

"Not long enough in the tooth?" I pulled the phone away from my now wrinkled face. I stared at it for a moment as if it were broken or the guy on the other end was crazy. If you Google "long in the tooth," it means, "Getting on in years, old, as in 'Aunt Aggie's a little long in the tooth to be helping us move.' This expression alludes to a horse's gums receding with age and making the teeth appear longer." My colleague's panel recommended a candidate with more years of experience than Sarah Manches, but a wild approach to leadership is to choose talent over experience.

> If a candidate has a sound, working level of experience for a job, choose talent for the long-term good rather than experience for the short-term gain.

I predicted that Sarah Manches, the most talented of my three finalists, might have a first year of productivity that trailed what the other two top candidates would achieve the first year, but would be on par with them the second year, and by the third year her talent would have her further along in development and success than the other two. I believed it was good for me and great for the larger organization to take that approach. The challenge was that the other two top candidates were excellent as well. One was age 41, with 20 years of experience, and the other 57, with more than 35 years of experience. Sarah had just 13 years of experience and was only 34 years old! She would be the youngest person on my leadership team to help guide more than 700 employees. To make the decision I thought about what the authors said in *First, Break All the Rules*: the old approach is to hire for experience and have someone hit the ground running. The new approach is to select for talent, define the right outcomes, focus on strengths, and find the right fit.[11] Well, 13 reference checks and 3 rounds of interviews later, I selected Sarah. By her second year, I saw that she could do not only her job expertly, but she could also do my job just as well. She could do my boss' in just a matter of time. As much as I wanted to keep Sarah around, after only 18 months, I encouraged her to apply for a leadership role in our national office. She was wisely picked by someone who also saw her talent. Two years after that she was selected for an even higher-level position. She wasn't yet the same age as the younger of the two candidates I considered against her. Sarah had talent. I have more than a dozen work stories like that, but I'll share just one more from my time as a youth sports coach.

Keith was confused when I said what players I wanted for our 13 and 14-year-old A-Team all-star baseball team. I trusted Keith's opinion as my top assistant coach for a long summer of ball games against some of the best teams north of Atlanta. However, I knew the boys better, having coached in that league for several years. Keith was further confused with my selections after he watched the first practice of the B-Team, supposedly the lesser talented of the two all-star teams to represent our league. He said that the majority of them were larger 14-year-olds, and some had facial hair. The B-Team players, on average, threw the baseball harder and hit the ball further. Our A-Team had seven 13-year-olds and just five 14-year-olds. "Trust me, Keith" was all I could say at that point, and Keith did to some extent. The previous season Keith and I coached, our team won the regular season title and also the postseason tournament. However, this was all-star season, and we would be facing the best competition in the northern one-third of Georgia. By the middle of our second tournament our record was 0 wins and 5 losses. At that point, I owed Keith a better explanation, especially as his frustration visibly grew. His son was one of the five 14-year-olds, and this would be his last youth all-star opportunity. I'm certain they didn't want to spend a long, hot summer only losing. I further explained: "Keith, I've watched all of these kids, both ages in this cohort, for several years now. I picked each one for a reason. Our team overall has less experience than the B-Team, but we have more talent. Also, they are all hard-working, respectful kids who get along well with others and will think more of the team first than themselves. Several of B-Teamers have bad

124

attitudes, and I believe the majority are at the talent ceiling for their age. Our boys will catch up fast." That bought me a little more time with Keith. Together with the other coaches we poured everything we had as leaders, mentors, and baseball strategists into those boys. The wins piled up. Not unlike the plot of a good sports movie, the summer crescendo was a face-off with our rivals from Kennesaw, Georgia, who beat us in all four previous meetings. Through the gauntlet of our schedule of dozens of games, we had to face Kennesaw three more times to win the title. There would be no better measure of our progress than to play the same team again later in the summer. We beat them all three times, topped off with the final showdown in the District Championship. We beat them 7-0. The B-team started the summer with more experience, and so did Kennesaw. We had talent. The experience came with time. So did the championship trophy.

True stories? Yes. Short on details of how to hire or select a team? Yes. Therefore, what follows, is more on…

HIRE HOW-TOS

The people we hire are our greatest contribution at work. There's not a practice, protocol, policy, or program that will last long after we leave. Sometimes others wait no later than the Monday after our Friday retirement party to drastically change our decisions 180 degrees. Yet, when we hire someone, that decision lasts years to decades. And when we hire managers and supervisors, who in turn hire others, we set in motion an impact that lasts decades to perhaps a hundred years or more.

Maybe you have done as I did in my less effective past: for short-term efficiency we make a quick pick and don't give much thought to the Big Four in our selections. We only call the three references (that they provide mind you), and not call three times that amount as we should. Sometimes that approach works out okay.

However, often it does not. I edited this section literally the day after I spent two hours with an attorney and a human resources representative to prepare for my testimony related to an employee's removal. Many hours, days, and weeks more were spent up to that point. I wish that the supervisor had spent a few more hours on reference checks for this employee, and I wish I would have ensured that they did.

In later chapters we will cover the value of doing "C-" work to enable "A" work where priorities matter most. Our efforts to hire the best, however, should always be A+.

Let's spend the time to do it right. The time it takes to select employees can be thought of in terms of literal minutes, hours, days, weeks, months, years, and decades in the following way:

If we take only minutes to hours to make selections—instead of more careful review of days to weeks—we will spend months to years with Human Resources and attorneys.

If you hire people that sentence may be among the most important words you read in this book. As important as the three r's of reading, writing, and 'rithmatic were in school is how important the four r's below are when we hire people.

1. **Recruit**. Recruiting can be done well by an outside firm or an internal group, but it's done best when we do it ourselves. Recruiting can be done by way of social media posts, email, and snail mail, but is best done face to face or by video call. We don't wake up one day and decide to recruit; we are on the lookout every day. We never stop looking for and attracting talent. We recruit in the middle of meetings, between conference sessions in the hallway, and when washing hands in the bathroom. I will take great liberty with the famous Winston Churchill speech— when he was focused on his most important task—and

change the word *fight* to *recruit*, the first step of our most important task:

> *we shall recruit on the seas and oceans,*
> *we shall recruit with growing confidence and growing*
> *strength in the air we shall recruit whatever the cost*
> *may be,*
> *we shall recruit on the beaches,*
> *we shall recruit on the landing grounds,*
> *we shall recruit in the fields and in the streets,*
> *we shall recruit in the hills;*
> *we shall never surrender.*

2. **Resume.** Not to be confused with the verb *resume* which rhymes with *assume*. Let us use the noun resume (which rhymes with *make you pay*) to represent all documents we should never assume has all the information we need. Like when we recruit, we must get personally engaged in resume reviews. A wild approach to leadership is to not look at what's in the resume, however. Look instead for what's missing. Are there:

   - unexplained gaps in time?
   - oddly brief stints?
   - reductions in pay from one job to another?
   - omissions of supervisors' names and contact numbers?
   - scant uses of the word "we," as if the candidate did everything alone?
   - no traces of volunteer work to serve the greater good?

There could be very good reasons for why those things are not there, but it is our job to find out why.

3. **Rally**. Let us use this action-oriented "r" word to say we need many people to rally to the cause for the interview stage. Rally more than just the candidates and the selecting official, as the final decision is strengthened with additional perspectives. The word "interview" can be broken down into "inter" or "interaction" and "view" or "perspectives". Let's maximize the interaction to maximize the perspectives to best understand the candidate. A strong, diverse interview panel we rally can help us see past our blind spots and biases. And don't stop at just one interview. In the hundreds of selections I have made or approved, the decision was much clearer after a second or third round of interviews. If you can only have one round, make it long and painful, or at least get into specifics. Patrick Lencioni wrote that, "Too many interviews are so generic that they provide little or no insight into specific attributes. Instead, they leave interviewers with extremely general assessments of candidates. 'She seems like a nice person. I like her.' That would be fine if you are looking for someone to mow your lawn once a week."[58]

4. **Reference checks**. Job application document reviews and interviews are indeed critical but should conceptually be no more than 49% of the overall evaluation. At least 51% of the decision to hire someone should be based on robust reference checks. Not just the 3-5 people the candidate lists on the application—which can include personal friends and relatives—call another order of magnitude; call 13-15 people and *go wide* and *deep*:

   - *Go wide* into the candidate's current organization—call their boss and that person's boss; call employees they supervise; call office

128

mates and other work colleagues; and, perhaps most insightful of all if you can get them on the phone, call the janitor and ask how well the candidate treated them.

- *Go deep* into the candidate's past—repeat the above step as far back in the past as possible. As you go deep into their past, many begin to forget specifics about the candidate. However, almost everyone will remember how the candidate made them feel, or they may dig up one single gold nugget that seals the deal on the candidate one way or another.

The first six sections of this chapter, "People," have covered what we look for in potential candidates and how to conduct effective hiring. If we get those pieces right, everything else is easier. The last four sections of this chapter cover how we effectively lead the people already in our organization, whether we hired them or inherited them. We will discuss how to deal with performance and conduct issues, but we can minimize those issues if we first ask ourselves: Are our people on the...

RIGHT SEAT ON THE BUS?

Tom rose through the ranks of my organization, from entry level to top senior staff. He was smart, organized, hard-working, and ambitious. He leveraged all of that into a series of technically focused jobs, with promotions and more responsibilities at each step. However, none of them included experience as a supervisor. Before I arrived, I had heard whispers of problems with Tom. Whispers became emails, and emails became memos. Ultimately, an independent report was placed on my desk. It detailed serious problems with Tom as a supervisor.

"With that many skills, how did he fail?" I asked. We failed him. Tom received scant preparatory leadership, management, or even supervisory training in his 15 years with us. He was not provided any developmental details to see if he might like or be good at supervising other employees.

All employees, if for no other reason than to be better followers, should receive some level of training in leading others. This will also grow the supervisor and manager candidate pool.

At some point, every supervisor was once a new supervisor with no experience, so we should train and develop our team to give a chance to succeed from the start. It was already too late for Tom in his current position. His tumultuous first year ended the sad day I sat across from him—and next to a Human Resources representative—to explain that he would move to a nonsupervisory position in another branch. I thought of what the authors of *First, Break All the Rules* said about otherwise great employees in the wrong job: "The best way to help an employee cultivate his talents is to find him a role that plays to those talents."[11] What happened after that with Tom was one of my great joys in witnessing a career resurrection. We moved Tom to the right seat on the bus. He then embraced the critical feedback provided. Still just as smart, organized, hard-working, and ambitious as ever, he applied those traits to his new role, as well as an array of supervision and leadership training our organization offered, a personal mentor I assigned, some courses we helped pay for, and several short-term then longer-term assignments that included supervising others. I gave him constant feedback along the way. Close to 10 years from the day we first sat across the table, we gathered by video conference to discuss his final performance review a month before his retirement. He received a "superior" rating in the element that dealt with people, and an overall "outstanding" rating, the highest of his career. Though Tom never became an official supervisor again, he became a national leader in his field and led people in other ways.

Tom was just one story. I could tell at least four more like it. They were all success stories once in the right seat on the bus, but all took great effort by the employees, their supervisors, and others. A big struggle each time was to know how much to develop what they were already good at, versus how much time to spend on improvements needed. To help answer that question let us consult...

ACHILLES HEEL AND PARETO'S PRINCIPLE

"Do I build on strengths or improve weaknesses?" We ask that question about our employees, our teams, and ourselves. A wild approach to leadership is to learn from the Achilles story and draw on Pareto's principle to help decide. But not the two men themselves; one isn't even real.

Achilles was the greatest of warriors in Greek mythology. His only physical vulnerability was his heel. That's where his mother held him as an infant to dip him in the river Styx, which had miraculous powers. An Achilles heel is today considered a weakness that debilitates despite an overall strength. Vilfredo Pareto was an Italian economist who coined the term "80/20 rule" while at the University of Lausanne in 1896. He showed that 80% of land in Italy was owned by 20% of the population. A management consultant named Joseph M. Juran then applied this to other things and named it the Pareto Principle. A thought in the business world is that 80% of the sales come from 20% of the clients. In sports some believe that 20% of good habits and exercises have 80% of the impact.

Let us ask the question again: "Do I build on strengths or improve weaknesses?" The answer is yes to both. That's the easy part. The hard part is to know how much to build on strengths versus try to improve weaknesses. A conventional approach to supervision and

131

management is to focus most on a weakness and improve it, whether that be the weakest 20% of our workforce or the weakest 20% of our own traits. A new, wilder approach, explained well by the authors of *First, Break All The Rules*, is for managers to recognize that, "…there is a limit to how much remolding they can do to someone…do not believe that everyone has unlimited potential…Don't waste time trying to put in what was left out. Try to draw out what was left in…Help each person become more of who he already is."[11] Wally Bock wrote that, "Dealing with weaknesses is important, but you don't want to make the mistake of trying to eliminate them. That usually takes too much time…Make them irrelevant."[70]

When I led adults during the workday and coached youth after work, I experienced the greatest returns when I invested 80% of my time and energy into my top 20% performers. When I was an athlete myself (or, more accurately, when I played sports, as I could hardly be described as an athlete) I applied this principle unknowingly. My high school basketball team was really good, but I wasn't. I was okay. Our team was ranked #1 in the state of Florida during my junior year and went to the state championship game my senior year. I loved basketball and wanted to contribute, but I ran slower and jumped lower than almost everyone else, certainly slower and lower than the starting five players. However, my coach named me the "sixth man"—the first one off the bench to substitute in the game. I earned this role through an intensive focus on my best asset: coordination. I spent extra hours in the gym and worked on my long-range, three-point shot, and I strived to perfect my mid-ranger jumper on the dirt court in my yard. If I had instead spent evenings and weekends sprinting and doing leg weights to help my horizontal speed and vertical jump, I would have at best improved to average on my team due to my limited genes.

For those of you like me who've tried to improve the bottom 20% in the workplace, it usually results in more time with Human Resources and attorneys than time enjoying our team's improvement.

While we invest 80% of our energy on our top 20% of performers, we must also address the Achilles heel(s).

Rather than attempt a broad fix for the bottom 20%, take a measured, more surgical approach. Deal with the one. When we deal with the one, we impact the many. This could look like a restructure or removal of the Achilles heel branch or office that drags down the organization's bottom line, or it could look like the reassignment or removal of a person. Despite our best efforts to hire the best, get employees on the right seat on the bus, and focus 80% of our energy on the best 20% employees, there will be employees who persist with serious issues of...

PERFORMANCE AND CONDUCT

"Do you know what happens when you keep a jackass longer than you should? The non-jackasses start to leave." –Patrick Lencioni[58]

Consistent with the 80-20 rule, in the first eight sections of this people-focused chapter we covered different angles of a leader's most important work: hire the best. If we get that right, all else is better and easier. But we don't always get that right—we make mistakes—and we often inherit the mistakes of others. Therefore, the last two sections in this chapter focus on a leader's second and third in priorities: deal with serious performance and conduct issues and personally engage as a coach and mentor.

Have you heard the following philosophical question? "If a tree falls in the woods and no one is around to hear it, does it make a sound?" I say it doesn't matter, but what does is the answer to the following question: "If an employee performs poorly or demonstrates poor conduct—and we did *not* write it down—did it happen?" The answer would get unanimous agreement between Human Resources, our attorney, their attorney, and the judge: no, it did not happen.

Dan Polles was a nice guy. He was one of two employees I supervised in my first manager position. I didn't think Dan would be a problem after my first week on the job. He was polite and submissive, and started every project I assigned. By the second week, however, I noticed that Dan didn't actually ever finish anything. More than that, he either arrived drunk or drank alcohol on the job. He also stole things. What ability I had as a new manager to direct, coach, and counsel was tested. I did not do well, but I did get to know Human Resources. Dan's removal became the only option. Poor performance documentation takes a long time, and it was difficult to gather clear evidence of either Dan's drunkenness or his thievery, as Dan was smart as well as nice. Frustrating as it was and unfair as it felt, if I could not document and write down Dan's issues, they did not happen. What was written down, however, was his timesheet. I ultimately fired Dan on a clear, documented discrepancy between when he said he worked and when he actually worked—not for being drunk on the job and stealing things.

What about the other 95 out of every 100 times we deal with less clear-cut conduct or performance issues? At the risk of sounding like a diet or exercise commercial, I offer you the eight-step approach to healthy supervision below. What follows is not a fool-proof plan, but an approach that enabled me, with increased success over 30 years, to improve dozens of employees' performance or conduct—or to fire the jackasses. That said, let us take an important pause:

The foundation of success is to start with a sincere heart to help people, to improve their conduct and performance at work, which often impacts the rest of their life.

Many employees, when provided clear direction and accountability, choose the proper path. For those who don't, it is emotionally taxing for us when we care about our employees as people and workers—to not feel responsible for their choice. Our job, however, is to provide proper direction and document the path that they (the employees, not us) choose. Though we are not responsible for their choices, we are indeed responsible to address the consequences of their actions. Should our employees choose not to improve their performance or conduct, we make it our problem, so it doesn't become everyone's problem.

Depending upon the number of different issues and the seriousness of the performance or conduct issue(s), we can certainly skip down one or many, though often it is a step-by-step approach. As frustrating as it may be to go slow and stop at each step, our results to improve employees are better or our case is stronger. The better we do at steps 1 and 2, the less likely we are to advance to step 3 and beyond.

1. Make expectations clear from day one

    → review the organizations mission and vision statements and the employee's position description initially and then annually, but, more importantly…

    → consider a personalized letter of expectation to explain what high-integrity conduct and successful performance looks like.

    → develop an annual work plan that is reviewed at least quarterly.

2. Provide personal feedback at least weekly

    → public and private praise for good work and private counsel when issues arise.

    → better than by email, text, or instant message is by phone, videoconference, or in person.

    → this is the most important step.

3. Document first-time issues informally

→ after a conversation with an employee, write a note or short memo to self and place it in what some call an unofficial "drop file;" empty that file at least annually if no further issues were noted.

4. Deal with a repeat issue with a "memo of counseling"

→ provide a written memo to the employee with a summary of expectations and previous guidance not followed; this is the last informal step that does not go in employee's official files.

5. Respond to a third issue with an official "memo of warning"

→ with this third strike, and certainly any subsequent steps, we work with our organization's human resources, personnel, and/or employee/labor relations staff (aka "HR") for their advice and their review of our written documents; this memo is retained in the employee's official file for a duration up to one year.

6. Elevate a fourth issue with more serious "letter of reprimand"

→ this step and step 5 are considered one in the same in some organizations, and one of them is often skipped, dependent upon the seriousness of the infraction; this memo is retained in the employee's official file for at least one year, often two years.

7. Suspend the employee with a fifth issue

→ the employee's last chance and the last step before removal; suspensions often range from one to thirty days, depending upon the seriousness of the issue; involve or at least inform our organizations' legal counsel in addition to HR at this step and the next, final step.

8. Remove the employee

> → after five chances to correct their performance or
> conduct issues, we can be confident in the employee's
> decision—not our decision—in their termination,
> separation, firing, removal, or whatever our
> organization calls it.

These eight steps are a general guide. They are, admittedly, a gracious, forgiving approach; your organization may be stricter. If followed step-by-step, though, with proper documentation along the way, we can have a clear conscience and clear case for our attorney to make. Whether we are dealing with the very worst employee or the very best—or any single person in between—they all deserve prompt and honest feedback. There's a way to do that right, and it's important that we…

DON'T SANDWICH IT

Feedback is more that "food for thought." It is essential nourishment for success. However, many of us were taught to provide that feedback food in a nice little sandwich: we say something nice first, then say something critical, then we close with something nice again. Truth is that's bologna. The real meat is lost if we mix messages.

If you need more sustenance than a food analogy, perhaps math might help explain. A negative and a positive of the same value when combined has a net result of zero. For example, $-1 + 1 = 0$ and $-3 + 3 = 0$.

Positive feedback right before negative feedback—or vice-versa—provides no net gain. Either the warm after-glow of a good compliment gets extinguished, or the needed sting of criticism gets softened. The sting is necessary.

British Prime Minister Winston Churchill said that, "Criticism may not be agreeable, but it is necessary. It fulfills the same function as pain in the human body. It calls attention to an unhealthy state of things."

We must also separate positives and negatives in space as well as time. That is, praise in public and criticize one-on-one. Criticism is most effective, as well as kind, when received as soon and as private as possible. When we catch someone in the act of doing something well, let us tell everyone and tell everyone right away—an instance when it's okay to talk behind someone's back. However, most powerful is a sincere compliment offered in person.

Three-time Superbowl champion coach Bill Walsh said, "Nothing is more effective than sincere, accurate praise, and nothing is more lame than a cookie-cutter compliment." How do we do that, though? In *The Carrot Principle*, the authors note that, "general praise has no impact." No employee wants to feel like a rabbit chasing after a one-size-fits-all prize. Carrots must be personalized."[24] I learned how to do that from a very personal and unlikely source: my father.

Arne Vego Viker left home when I was six, and I only saw him once or twice a year after that. When I did see him, he did not speak much. He was a quiet man with a low, deep voice. So, when he did speak, I listened carefully. My dad worked for many supervisors over his four decades as a mechanic. Dad told me once in his thick Brooklyn accent: "I noah good bawz when I see one." Wanting to be a good boss myself one day, I pressed dad for more. He said that promotions, awards, and more money each week in his paycheck "ain't that great over the long haul." He said what inspired him the most was when he knew that his work mattered and that he was appreciated for it. It must be both. Equally unhelpful and demoralizing is when: (a) we're told that we're good at a job, but not that it makes a difference; or (b) that our work is meaningful, but we believe we are not good at it. If the work of our team member matters and they make a difference, let us say so—and do so in a timely manner. Imagine the impact on your child if you said, "You are punished. Go to your room!" The child asks why, and you say, "Because back in February, maybe either the second or third Saturday I think, you didn't clean your room." What if we patted our dog's head and fed a mouth-watering biscuit for his potty habits two weeks ago, yet unbeknownst to us, Fido just watered the patio chair cushion with urine. Guess what Fido will do again?

Gallup survey expert Tom Rath said that "Employees who report receiving recognition and praise within the last seven days show increased productivity, get higher scores from customers, and have better safety records. They're just more engaged at work." We make feedback effective by frequency and *in*formality, not *in*frequency and formality. My favorite of Dan Rockwell's, "10 simple ways to improve performance conversations" are to increase frequency to at least twice a month, decrease formality, and shorten the length.[13] Let us also avoid the scattered feedback sandwiches and instead provide a steady diet of timely effective praise or correction. Executive Coach Ed Batista advised us to, "Make feedback normal. Not a performance review."

All that said, I estimate that at least 90% of organizations still require a formal, written performance evaluation at least annually. Exactly 100% of them, however, should begin with something like the following unconventional—if not wild approach—remarks:

"I promise that there will never be any surprises when we do these performance evaluations. You are always safe with me. This past year as you accomplished things or did things well, I hope I have always shared my gratitude and other feedback with you. Know too that I've talked behind your back in a good way to other people. If you have done something this past year that I have been less pleased with, I have always kept it between the two of us and we discussed it soon after. Again, there are no surprises when we do performance evaluations. You are always safe with me. This meeting is to hear your reflections about learning and growing this past year through your successes and challenges."

The dreaded performance evaluation should never be dreaded, nor even an evaluation, so much as it is a recap of the employee *by the employee* of what they learned throughout the year. We are there to walk alongside them and hold the lantern.

At this point in the book we have built on *who we are*—in terms of the four Cs of connection, character, collaboration, and communication—and moved through *what we do* with it, starting with the most important piece: people. But now what? As my grandma used to say, "don't just stand there, do something." We've gathered a great team; now, we must make good decisions happen.

CHAPTER 6

Policy — Make It Happen

INTRODUCTION

The word policy sounds boring. Why then did I choose policy to be the one-word summary for this chapter? The answer is simple: It starts with the letter "P," and I thought I had a clever thing going with the whole four "Cs" and the four "Ps" thing. I really just couldn't think of a better "P" word. Policy works, though, if we do it the right way.

Last generation's hard cover dictionary and this generation's Google agree that the word policy describes a variety of decisions that guide our actions, including law, regulation, procedure, and practice. Let us not think of policy as only the stuff written in three-ring binders or an organization's intranet site. For the purposes of this chapter and going forward, let's equate policy with making good decisions happen, whether written or spoken.

This chapter begins with the end in my mind, so let's get to the bottom line without further ado:

For good decisions to happen, we must take steps to make them happen.

Leadership expert Andy Stanley says that "Direction, not intention determines your destination." Good decisions don't happen on their own, and they are not the result of good intention. We must execute. Before we tell someone else what to do, however, we must first...

BOSS OURSELVES AROUND

My wife gets understandably exasperated about my lack of short-term memory. She told me that I forget what I eat for breakfast each morning, and then quickly added, "And you eat the same thing every day!" (It is bran flakes, and she is right). We humans are a forgetful species. Sometimes we conveniently forget things, so plot against yourself in advance and hard wire your intentions into actions. For example, block your path out the front door with the empty laundry basket to remind you to move the clothes from the washer to the dryer.

My youngest son knew to feed his pet fish whenever he brushed his teeth and knew to brush his teeth when he fed his fish. Don't ask me to explain it. Ask him. I do know this: it worked for him. Even if we don't have the best memory, no one else knows us like we know ourselves, so let's use that information to our advantage. A wild approach to leadership is to boss ourselves around, every single day, and do it in writing if needed.

I keep an old-fashioned to-do list in my pocket, and I also set alarms on my phone to remind me to do something. Speaking of alarms, do we want to be more likely to exercise in the morning? Let us set our alarm to wake 45 minutes early, and conveniently set out our tee shirt, shorts, and running shoes—and not our work clothes. How do I start my day with a healthy meal and be less likely to grab a donut? I pre-set the morning breakfast table with, um, uh, oh, yeah: bran flakes. We must find unique ways that work for us to make change easy for ourselves and others.

> Why is that at meetings when there's fruit on the table near the coffee, people always grab the bananas first and not the oranges? Bananas are easy.

As Tania Luna and Jordan Cohen wrote: "Want certain people to talk more? Seat them close together …Want people to do more brainstorming? Put up whiteboards or have stacks of Post-It Notes in every room…want people to recycle more? Place large bins in various spots around the office…So, next time you are tempted to convince someone (or even yourself) to change a behavior, consider how you might change the friction level instead."[43]

In the middle of a hiring freeze in the early 1990s, I was prematurely thrust into a supervisory and management role at the age of 23. I was ill-prepared. My wildlife ecology, botany, and forestry courses were of little help, and chemistry, physics, and calculus offered no additional insights on dealing with people. So, I started to read a wide array of books about leadership. My problem was time was scarce. I worked 45-50 hours per week, then I was a newlywed, then I had a young family, then a house to clean, a yard to maintain, and youth sports teams to coach after work and before supper. Never mind exercise or down time. Sound familiar? My story is probably not too unlike yours. I needed and wanted to grow my leadership skills, but didn't have a half-hour to spare, much less an hour. How did I do it? I hard-wired reading into my life in quarter-hour increments. In 15-minutes over bran flakes on most mornings, I amassed nearly 2,000 hours of reading and consumed around 150 books. Here's the math:

0.25 hours x 300 days x 28 years = 2,100 hours. It is not realistic for most of us to carve out large blocks of time to read, take a course, talk to a mentor, or otherwise study. We must take digestible bites. "A little improvement each day makes a big difference over time," said Tony Dungy, leadership author and professional sports coach. He advises us to, "Remember to focus on goals that are within your control."[69]

I love to challenge old adages, but there are some that resonate well with me. As a former federal game warden and wildlife biologist, I try to get past the image of the following, as it has a strong impact. Question: "How do you eat an elephant?" Answer: "Easy, one bite at a time." Large endeavors are made manageable when we take small, manageable steps. Hardwire the change. The freedictionary.com said that hardwiring something means, "To implement a capability through logic circuitry that is permanently connected ..." Though I don't know what logic circuitry is, I'm pretty sure I get what permanently connected is. If something is important to us, and we want the change to be permanent, then we should hardwire it into our life until it becomes habit. Bestselling author Jim Collins in *Good to Great* said that "Greatness, it turns out, is largely a matter of conscious choice, and discipline."[9] What's important to you? What do you want to hardwire into the circuitry of your life? Boss yourself around but make it easy. We must also make things easier on others. One way we make things unnecessarily hard is to have...

TOO MANY ON A TEAM

"The more, the merrier" is what I used to think, especially around the holidays. One mid-December day my wife was not pleased when I invited half the neighborhood (as she described it) to our home for a Christmas party. Gracious as always, Lulie was by no means the Grinch to our neighbors, but I did get coal in my stocking that year. I always underestimated—because I never fully understood—the work it took Lulie, the best cook I know, to prepare her famous feast.

At work I also overextended and overtaxed those I relied upon most when I formed teams. There wasn't a work group, task force, or committee I didn't make larger than it had to be. If ten folks raised their hand to volunteer for an effort—and I found that Shantel, Sam, and Sally also might want to join—I called it good at a baker's dozen. The problem was, time and again, I was oblivious to the wildly appropriate adage that too many cooks spoiled the stew. I thought the more the merrier, but I made it harder than it needed to be for those who did the heavy lifting, like my dear Lulie in the kitchen.

How many is too many cooks in a kitchen or members of a team? I never knew what number the right number for teams was, so I thought any number would do. Perhaps I unknowingly drew on my coaching experience. Rules in sports, more familiar to me, require 9 on a baseball diamond, 11 for football, and 11 for soccer. Maybe that's why so many of the teams I formed had 10 or more.

Ten on a team is a good, round, solid number, right? Wrong. Studies show that half that amount is better.

I should have thought more in terms of basketball and wish I would have read the well-researched book *Scrum* sooner. "The team dynamic only works well in small teams. The classic formula is seven people, plus or minus two." The authors went on to explain that "Data shows that if you have more than nine people on a team, their velocity actually slows down…Groups made up of three to seven people require about 25 percent of the effort of groups of nine to twenty to get the same amount of work done."[30] Indeed the number varies based on a number of factors. *Team of Teams* answer the question: "How many 'cooks' is too many? It depends. In a small kitchen or office four might be the ideal number. For a company with operations the size of

Walmart, the break point is much higher." However, as in *Scrum*, the author notes that, "As the proverbial kitchen fills up, communication and trust breaks down, egos come into conflict, and the chemistry that fueled innovation and agility becomes destructive." It is, "...a fallacy that bigger teams are better than smaller ones because they have more resources to draw on...as a team gets bigger, the number of links that need to be managed among members goes up at an accelerating, almost exponential rate."[17] Another way to look at team size is to follow billionaire Jeff Bezo's "two pizza rule." Bezos said that every internal team should be small enough that it can be fed with two pizzas. I guess that's where team composition then becomes the key consideration. For a team with my sons Dane and Matthew, there's room for maybe just one more.

Once we have the right team size, we must remain vigilant that members don't retreat into solo corners or huddle into small, exclusive groups. A sign of a cohesive team with productive, healthy conflict is the lack of pre-meeting strategizing or post-meeting venting behind closed doors. A healthy team has "the meeting within the meeting." The strategizing and venting happens by all, with all, and for the benefit of all. How do we do that? We...

BREAK IT ON PURPOSE

Worse than when someone said they had a beef with me was when my mom said, "I have a bone to pick with you." We don't hear that phrase often nowadays, but just know that it means conflict is about to happen. What I perceived as bad as a child, though, is a necessity and good thing in the adult workplace. That is, healthy conflict. Why do we assume good decisions only come from meetings with peace and harmony? In fact, if our meetings and workplace are too polite and agreeable, chances are the agreement is not for the best idea, rather the first idea, the easiest idea, or the boss' idea. In *Think*

Again, author Adam Grant noted that, "The absence of conflict is not harmony, it's apathy."[74] A wild approach to leadership is to mine for conflict, and, if there isn't any, create some. Intentionally throw a bone on the table to pick on and gnaw on. Try to break what you don't think needs fixing.

I fail as a leader when I fail to follow the words of General Colin Powell: "'If it ain't broke, don't fix it' is the slogan of the complacent, the arrogant or the scared…The job of a leader is not to be the chief organizer, but the chief dis-organizer." The authors of *The Practice of Adaptive Leadership* said it more academically but nonetheless helpfully: "Orchestrating conflict requires courage…tolerating the moments your people are not working well together, and believing that working through some rough patches will help to solidify their collective effort and commitment…Orchestrating conflict requires tolerating a high degree of conflict yourself, perhaps more than you are comfortable with…"[22]

The author of *The 3rd Alternative* reminds us that, "…an organization is full of conflict because it has a job to do, and every creative, thoughtful, talented, exceptional human being in the organization has different insights into how to do that job. Those insights are contradictory, baffling, quirky, and inconsistent; they can also be useful or even brilliant."[47] A particularly healthy leadership team I worked with once wisely invested time to develop and post the following in a public place:

<u>5 Rules for Productive Teams</u>:
1. Allow time for healthy conflict.
2. Engage in candid, frank discussions.
3. Be all-inclusive of opposing views.
4. Respect different communication styles.
5. Actively solicit opposing viewpoints.

Why again do we do this? We want to make the best decisions possible. Decisions don't make themselves, certainly not great ones. The five points above can be quite helpful. If we forgot one or more of them, it won't be the end of the world. It may not even mean the end of the meeting. It will be though if we don't...

SHUT UP IN BETWEEN

If you think this provocatively titled section could go in the communication chapter of this book, you would be right. It could go there. It should also go here. As leaders we often impede good policy—the development and execution of a good decisions—by simply opening our mouth. Have you watched a television show or movie where a workplace scene centers around a conference room table and the boss talks constantly or barks orders to a disengaged or shell-shocked staff? Sadly, the real world is not too different. Consider another way, a wildly different and effective approach to leadership, where the boss opens a meeting, closes a meeting, and shuts up in between.

In the next section, Seal the Deal, we will cover how an effective leader opens a meeting with the *why* and closes the meeting with *who* will do *what* by *when*. This section is the essential approach of doing nothing in between, and that's at least for a couple reasons. First, the leader cannot listen and talk at the same time. We can't learn from others while we ourselves are sharing. Though we are designed to walk and talk—and some (not I) can walk, talk, and chew gum—not a one of us can process things from others while we talk. It is no coincidence that the very first section in this book is about how we have two ears and one mouth.

The second reason that leaders should shut up in between is that the moment a leader speaks, no matter how well they caveat their input, it will be taken by many as the final decision or at least the way the leader now leans. The more we speak as leaders, the more we narrow the scope of the conversation in others' minds.

The team's creativity will be diminished if not vanquished as team members begin to think of ways to implement the leader's one idea rather than consider the best of all ideas. So much is lost when that happens.

It is true that once in a rare while the leader is the smartest, most creative person in the room. But even then, that one person's idea, however brilliant, is not as good as the combined energy and ideas of many.

I am terrible at meeting facilitation when at the same time I am supposed to be the decision maker. At my best I usually fail to reign in my passion for a topic, and sometimes, less noble, my ego or need for control comes in play. We cannot serve as both facilitator of the discussion and ultimate decision maker or both roles will suffer—and one is not our job! For the energetic, extroverted, unbridled enthusiastic among us, I know it is hard to stay quiet when we care so deeply. Let us remember, though, that our team members care deeply too, so let's hear them out. The best decision will come after—not before—getting all the ideas on the table.

In the book *The Work of Leaders* the authors wrote: "Remaining open doesn't mean you're indecisive...It's not that you can't make up your mind—it's about not making a decision too early."[53] Let's also consider the advice of David Cote, chairman and chief executive of Honeywell: "Your job as a leader is to be right at the end of the meeting, not at the beginning of the meeting."

We start with good intention, but we must end with great execution for decisions to actually be implemented. We will cover that next. If you would allow me, to ensure proper execution, let's transition with three clichés in succession: we must close the loops, wrap it up, and...

SEAL THE DEAL

My cousin Kevin was a gift wrapper of infamy in our family. Kevin would intentionally, unnecessarily, and exhaustively wrap every Christmas present. I imagine that he would cast back his long, red, untamed hair and laugh wildly before he leaned in, hunched over, and set Christmas chaos in motion in his dank and dimly lit basement. I wager my cousin spent more money on Scotch tape, green ribbon, and red wrapping paper than on the gifts themselves. He over-wrapped every present to everyone and every year. However, in 1982, Kevin wrapped one too many layers one too many times. His uncle, my father, plotted revenge. My dad purchased an expensive adjustable wrench he knew Kevin wanted. Dad also bought a short length of thick metal pipe that would fit the wrench snuggly inside it. Dad then welded both ends of the pipe to permanently seal the wrench inside. Then, before he neatly concealed the pipe in one simple layer of wrapping paper, dad drilled a hole in the pipe just big enough for Kevin to see his new adjustable wrench, but not actually be able touch it, hold it, or use it—ever. That Christmas was the hardest I'd seen Kevin laugh my entire life.

Dad literally sealed the fate of Kevin's wrench before it was ever unwrapped, and, in doing so, altered the course of our Christmases to come. Similarly, we set the course then fate of our decisions most during wrap-up and not in the delivery. We seal the deal—that is, end the meeting and set great decisions in motion— when the most critical question is completely answered during wrap-up: *who* will do *what* by *when?*

Until we are all clear who is responsible, what they will do, and when it needs to be done, our decisions will be executed wrong, late, or not at all.

As leaders we are at our best when we start with the *why*—the purpose—and avoid the *how, where, and which* details that are best left to subject matter experts in the middle of the meeting. Leaders, however, have an essential role during wrap up to ensure the critical accountability of *who* will do *what* by *when*. The author of *Team of Teams* suggests that leaders can't empower then walk away. They must provide tools and the best information. "An organization should empower its people, but only after it has done the heavy lifting of creating shared consciousness."[17] That shared consciousness—and every good meeting and every good decision—starts with the *why* and ends with *who* will do *what* by *when*.

My 30 years of experience, informed by many failures as a producer, supervisor, manager, then leader, has proven that 90% of successful execution is not in the doing, rather being clear what must be done, who will do it, and when it is due. The remaining 10% of execution consists of details that usually work themselves out. However, 100% of the time, don't have…

MORON MEETINGS

No I didn't misspell the title. Though this section is indeed *more on* meetings, the first piece of advice is to not have *moron* meetings. We, fortunately, don't hear the word moron as much as last century. "You're such a moron!" exclaimed Billy Murray, my first cousin, when we were in fourth grade. I dreamed I accidentally locked Billy's bike to mine instead of the bike rack and then both bikes were stolen.

To be sure I used the term correctly this century for illustrative purposes, I unlocked my bike, peddled four miles to the library, and asked the librarian if he had a dictionary to look up the word moron. No, I didn't. Only a moron would do that. Instead, I just typed moron in Google and found one short definition: "a stupid person." So, then I Googled the word stupid, and the definition was "Having or showing a great lack of intelligence or common sense."

So, do you want to have moron meetings—meetings showing a great lack of intelligence or common sense? Have no purpose. Meet just to meet. Schedule a time annually, monthly, weekly, daily, or just once, and have no purpose. That moronic approach, however, is not to be confused with an unstructured meeting to personally connect with one another. Those are okay. There's a purpose in that—to connect—and that is critically important time spent for teams as a whole and individuals that comprise them. Though such bonding sessions are inefficient short term, they result in a more effective team long term.

There are a lot of wild approaches to have effective impromptu or periodic meetings. Several ways are featured below, and you likely have several more ideas. Note that there is one universal *never* included.

It is okay to…
  …meet for just five or ten minutes,
  …not make the meeting place comfortable,
  …cover only one topic, and
  …have no agenda,
but it's *never* okay to have no purpose.

Television and movies also often portray meetings as classroom style gatherings. The boss is the teacher who does all the talking, and the employee are like students who sit in rows, either bored or distracted. I've attended some of those (and probably led some of those). A wild, more effective approach to break down literal and figurative walls is to shake up the room and have one large circle of chairs or groups of tables instead of rows. Have the different levels of staff or supervisory hierarchy and the different job disciplines or program all mixed in together. Have marketing sit alongside administrative staff and ask maintenance sit next to accounting. What may start as awkward pleasantries at first often builds toward rich interactions that solve problems in new ways.

Here's some more on meetings: Do you want an almost guaranteed way to slice your meeting time by at least one-third and maybe by two-third's time? Ask everyone to stand up and remain standing if they are able. Notice then how people will speak less frequently and more efficiently when they are less comfortable. This wild approach is quite appropriate when the meeting purpose is just to share information and ask for clarification, and not foster robust discussion. Why reduce meeting times when possible? We need more thinking time, which some have called "white space," like the margins around the edges of a book. Imagine if the words of a book literally started on the top left corner and letters and words ran nonstop until the bottom left with no white space. That's how our days would be without figurative white space. Clay Scroggins once asked, "Do I run my calendar or does my calendar run me? The worst is having a stack of meetings, back-to-back. While this can seem efficient, it can also be an enemy of critical thinking. I will get to the end of my day and realize I've generated no new thoughts, no new ideas."[63]

It is also okay to have no agenda. My mentor, Mark Musaus, described to me a most effective meeting he attended. It was not one with materials to review in advance, participants were given no time to prepare, and there wasn't an agenda. Mark and other officials learned upon arrival that the meeting did have a clear, compelling purpose. They were there to discuss a concealed weapons policy on federal lands. Mark said that as interesting as the topic was, the discussion during the meeting was not as memorable as the management of the meeting. He noted that it started promptly at 3:00 p.m., and it ended promptly at 4:00 p.m. The leader provided a brief introduction about the meeting's purpose, carefully listened to the discussion, and stayed quiet in between. Before the meeting ended, the leader asked each participant if there was anything else they wanted to say. The leader then summarized the discussion, noted the key points, assigned action items and deadlines, and thanked the participants. That doesn't sound like many meetings I have attended. How about you? To make our meetings, policies, and most importantly, our decisions more effective, there is great symbolic and practical value to…

SHOW IT SO THEY KNOW IT

Why do we have pictures of our loved ones on our desk? Why do we have our phone on a charger near them? Those people matter most to us, and we need it. When things matter and they are needed, they are displayed or kept handy.

There is both symbolic and practical value to post organization's mission statement or core values on the wall. Over time, though, they often blend in with the crown molding or seem to become invisible like ceiling fire extinguisher sprinklers. Sometimes the words of our mission statements are figuratively too lofty in the clouds, so they are literally not helpful on the ground.

How then can we display things that matter but also make them helpful? Make them relevant every day. One of the best examples I saw of practical guidance for meetings was in a U.S. Forest Service conference room. Posted alongside pictures of forestland was two large, matching, framed instructions on each side of the room that asked meeting participants:

1. What is happening right now that everyone needs to know?
2. What issues are occurring today that will affect the entire group?
3. What help is needed from others?
4. What are key results/outcomes of recent meetings/events?
5. What key meetings/events are planned for the coming days/weeks?

These federal tree professionals would *root* their conversations Monday mornings before they would *leaf* the room and *branch* out for the week (Sorry, I couldn't help it). Seriously now, they were indeed soundly rooted in what matters most for meetings. They had straightforward, relevant, and easily referenced questions to guide their discussions. These questions helped ensure meetings were both efficient and effective—focused on priorities

The best way to ensure a meeting goes well is to plan it in advance. Often that includes preparatory materials, but more often it involves conversations with the most influential person in the room that day, and that person is often not the boss. Let me tell you about the single most consequential public meeting I planned and led the first half of my career. Our team had to tell very wealthy and famous residents that we were going to remove all the trees they liked to look at and then burn what was left on the federal land near their property. Yes, you read that right. Remove the trees and burn what's left. The two key components of that type of wildlife habitat restoration project in a rare coastal scrub ecosystem was to remove taller shade trees and then intentionally light a fire known as a prescribed burn to remove underbrush. This would mimic what nature has done for thousands of years, and wildlife has adapted and benefitted. But that is what we wildlife biologists understood and try to explain. That's not what reached residents' ears. Most heard: "Cut down all trees and burn what's left." Others thought, "Never mind the critters. What about us?" This was the early 2000s and that slice of Florida coastline on Jupiter Island was considered the wealthiest community in America based on property value. Sports, movie, and music stars either lived or played there. The project land was in their view shed across a body of water, and right next to movie star Burt Reynolds' house.

I and the rest of the staff prepared for months. In the early days of PowerPoint presentations, we had a really good one. We practiced, and then we practiced again. Though I am sure we didn't do everything correctly to prepare for the big day, I am certain we did one thing right. We spoke to Nathaniel P. "Nat" Reed in advance. His family and some friends once owned the entire island, and slowly sold it to the rich and famous except for their estates. We explained to Nat what we wanted to do, and how there would be a short-term visual loss for a long-term wildlife habitat gain. It helped that Nat was once the Assistant Secretary for Fish, Wildlife and Parks under two presidents and helped write the Endangered Species Act. What helped more, though, was that he was known by all residents and well respected. When the meeting began, I and the rest of the team landed somewhere between very nervous and completely terrified. Although we thought the meeting would last one to two hours, it was over in less than 15 minutes. That was because Nat Reed stood up in the middle of the presentation we never finished, and eloquently offered his unsolicited opinion on the whole matter. No other attendees asked a question, nor offered an opinion. They didn't need to. Nat spoke. Then they all stood up, went home, and the project went forward. Nearly twenty years later, after Nat's passing and following an Act of Congress, I returned to that spot. As part of a formal ceremony, I gave a speech and then introduced United States Senator Connie Mack to help proclaim that land forever more the Nathaniel P. Reed National Wildlife Refuge. I was later asked what it was like to introduce a Senator. I replied that I was just glad to have met Nat Reed.

We have now completed several sections about meetings, a key part of making things happen. It is essential, however, not to stay in meetings too long, in your line of work or in this book. Let us step outside of the meeting space, breathe deeply, and consider that...

SMELLING IS BELIEVING

I couldn't decide whether to title this section "Smell It First" or "Seeing is Believing," so I settled on a minimally clever combination: "Smelling is Believing." Anyway...

Two armed federal security guards banged their clenched left hands on Dexter Soileau's door. Their right hands were anxious alongside their holsters. As they considered their pistols, Dexter, calm in his temporary apartment, contemplated who might have just knocked really hard. He sauntered to the door, relaxed, to greet his guests. Dexter was unaware of anything wrong with the long knife in his one hand, dripping blood, and the over-sized fork in the other. If his appearance wasn't alarming enough, the chopped, bloody corpse in the bathtub over his right shoulder was. One of the guards hollered, "Oh my God, they done kilt somebody!" Before the armed guards could draw their pistols, though, Dexter set out to convince them otherwise. "Look it's an alligator! Look, there's a tail!" Next Dexter's mouth drew a large smile and offered a warm invitation in his thick Cajun accent. "Ah, meh, y'all come on in and pass some time. I'm fryin' some alligator." Some things we must see for ourselves. No doubt the report the officers heard included sounds of struggle, glimpses through window blinds of knives and blood ... and a body! When in reality, Dexter, a federal game warden, was joyfully and legally preparing the latest package from home in the midst of a three-month schooling at the Federal Law Enforcement Training Center in southern Georgia. Dexter brought all his Cajun spices and cooking supplies with him from south Louisiana. His wife mailed him the meat on dry ice every few weeks. Sometimes it was crawfish (or crayfish to those north of Interstate 20), duck, deer, buffalo (the fish, not the bison), and that time, it was gator.

A wild approach to leadership is to *not* believe what we see. "I saw it with my own eyes" is rarely the final word on a subject.

Let us make important decisions only after we have engaged more of the senses in decision making. See things, smell things, feel things, and, if it won't make you sick, taste things. Good decisions are made after we gather essential ingredients, but too often we stop with just facts we see figures on paper, or words from other's mouths. What if we only punished little Johnny for what we saw him do to Sally's toy car? We might have pulled a wheel off too, if we found the left arm of our doll inside the car. It gets more serious, though.

A senior staff member I worked with saw with his own eyes ample evidence to accuse another of an alcohol problem. Many mornings, especially Mondays, he said this lady came to work with blood-shot eyes and signs of sleepiness. Her face was often red. The assumption was, especially on Mondays, that she drank way too much on the weekend. The truth was, however—which I saw for myself— that she spent nearly every weekend outdoors on ballfields for her children, often got sunburned, had severe allergies, and also struggled with sleep apnea.

Let us get out of the ivory tower and walk on the ground where the action is if we really want to know what's going on. In *Managing the Unexpected*, the authors write that, "...people in higher positions often get nothing but filtered good news, those senior people continue to believe that things are going well...But the first to know tend to be lower in rank, invisible, reluctant to speak up..."[56] If you are a youth sports coach, join the kids at practice and be a player in an intra-squad scrimmage. Are you the district manager of a chain of restaurants who heard the head chef needs new but expensive ovens? Take your tie off and put your apron on. A teacher might sit as a student in another class. A chief executive officer of a corporation could work alongside an entry-level employee on the front lines.

Let's get out on the ground from time to time and experience things ourselves. Get out of the office and see the front lines of your organization. Begin with General Colin Powell's initial assumption that, "The commander in the field is always right and the rear echelon is wrong, unless proved otherwise." When we listen to all the information from a variety of sources, we will have a painting more vivid—and valid—than our eyes ever could construct. Dexter wasn't butchering a body; the poor guy was just preparing supper.

Here's some food for thought: after we've seen things for ourselves and made a decision, that doesn't mean we need to do it ourselves. Though leaders are responsible for work, they are rarely best positioned to actually do the work. That's why it is critical for leaders to know when to personally produce, and what it means to either…

SUPERVISE, MANAGE, OR LEAD

Laura Brandt, at first glance, is not an imposing figure. She is barely over five feet tall, and maybe 95 pounds—and only when she steps on a scale in her alligator gear. Yes, alligator in a second straight story. Recall that this book is not titled, *Boring Office Stories Leadership*.

In the Everglades, Laura looms large in local lore as an alligator expert in this famed Florida wetland. She prefers you call her Laura, not Dr. Brandt, though she does have a PhD. Unassuming, Laura will back an airboat down the boat ramp herself; catch, measure, and tag an alligator with no help; and then wash the mud and muck off the airboat without assistance, though there are ample interns willing to lend a hand to impress a most impressive person.

Laura has been known to subdue an alligator at night with her bare hands, bake cookies for coworkers in the morning, tutor a disadvantage child after work, then beat a much younger racquetball opponent at night. Laura was a nationally ranked racquetball player, but she is not impressed with titles—hers or yours. She has explained Everglades issues to Presidential cabinet members, and all the major newspapers in south Florida have asked Laura for her perspective. She influenced countless decisions within her agency, and serves as a role model for sound science and work ethic into a fourth decade of her work career. Laura doesn't manage large sums of money nor land, and she supervises others only occasionally. However, Laura always leads.

You could be thinking right now: do I supervise, manage, or lead? You probably do all three at least a little each day. We often do, and probably should. We also must produce—do work ourselves and not just tell other people what to do. Many of us at some point in our workday are some combination of producer, supervisor, manager, or leader. Perhaps we should be aware of and be good at our multiple roles but let us be best at leadership.

There are many definitions of leadership, but the one that most resonates with me can apply to us all. John C. Maxwell, author of *The 21 Irrefutable Laws of Leadership*, said that "Leadership is influence, nothing more nothing less."[46] Laura Brandt has influence. Laura is a leader. Employees, supervisors, and managers are all leaders if they have influence.

A supervisor is simply one who is responsible for another's work, whereas a manager is responsible for people and other resources such as funds, supplies, equipment, buildings, and land. Leaders, in contrast, look for new resources and new ways of doing things.

A manager must be efficient in the short-term, using resources already in hand; however, a leader reaches out for new resources for long-term effectiveness.

John P. Kotter writes in *What Leaders Really Do*, that "Managers promote stability while leaders press for change…motivating and inspiring—keeping people moving in the right direction despite major obstacles to change…"[35].

Leadership guru Peter Drucker also equated efficiency to management and effectiveness to leadership, famously saying, "Efficiency is doing things right; effectiveness is doing the right thing." The consequences of a management focus, when leadership is needed, impacts a company's bottom line and can be a matter of life and death. Three days after Christmas in 1978, United Airlines Flight 173 crashed into a neighborhood, killing 10 on board. The crew was so focused on a landing gear issue that the plane ran out of fuel. Following the crash, one of the solutions the airline industry settled on was not more technical training. Instead, they, "…focused on group dynamics, leadership, interpersonal communications, and decision making…"[17]

The Flight 173 crew needed a Laura Brandt—someone to ask for a pause to what was considered *efficient* process to consider more creative, *effective* possibilities. That someone could have been captain or crew, manager or supervisor, or employee. Perhaps, to a person, each did not think it was their place. As leaders we must create an environment where everyone thinks it is their place. A wild approach to leadership is to give away authority at every turn. Great leaders must…

EMPOWER AND DELEGATE

We *think* we can do other people's jobs, but we often can't and usually shouldn't. Unlike the vast majority of aspiring singers and dancers on the first week of tryouts for *American Idol* and *So You Think You Can Dance*, we must first be completely honest with ourselves about our abilities. More than that, though, why not delegate specific tasks to others or empower in general? This will enable us to focus on what we alone can do and what we do best. We will then increase ownership and morale and build a stronger team for the future.

This chapter thus far has covered personal accountability, structure of teams, value of diverse thought, a reminder to listen, effective meetings, the value of first-hand experience, and knowing our role. There is no better way to end this chapter about how to make things happen than to close with empowerment and delegation. I think of these two similar concepts as a *heart-set* and a *mind-set*. To empower is to generally start with a heart to give away power or authority, an effective default approach for leaders. Delegation is a specific daily mindset to be intentional about assigning tasks that we could otherwise do. It frees us to focus on the highest and best use of our time. We'll cover this topic in more detail in the chapter on priorities. For now, helpful questions to ask ourselves:

Am I focused on the vital few or the useful many?
Is what I am doing right *now* that which *only* I can do?

We often think too highly of ourselves or don't understand effective management of the modern workforce. According to the authors of *Team of Teams* we should ensure that, 'Decisions are pushed downward, allowing members to act quickly. This new approach also requires changing the traditional conception of leader. The role of the leader becomes creating a broader environment instead of command-and-control micromanaging.'[17] Only do what we can do, and in both senses of the phrase. Let's not do someone else's job, and let's not do things we are not good at.

In my line of work, I relate to wildlife examples to help illustrate things. Again, from *Team of Teams*: "We envision an insect hierarchy, at the head sits the queen, organizing the labor and her minions and directing battles with rival populations. The truth is that the queen is a larva factory. Her sole job is to produce new ants—a critical role, but not a managerial one. The myth survives because of our assumption that order is always directed from the top down."

The most work is done, and the best ideas come most often from the bottom up—from the front lines to the front office. However, to take those ideas and to harness the efforts of the entire team, to remain effective for the long haul it often takes a little…

CHAPTER 7

Planning – Prepare For The Future

INTRODUCTION

The blue dot that blinks on many phone's map app shows us exactly where we are. The problem is, we think the blinking blue dot can magically take us where we need to be without fail. We never question it.

When our three children were still in school, the older two convinced us to visit a new church in an unfamiliar part of Atlanta. After the service, it took no convincing that the teenagers were hungry, so we piled in the family vehicle, and quickly agreed on a restaurant we saw advertised on a billboard. Amid the glass and steel of Atlanta, this place was a western lodge-styled restaurant, with big wooden beams and stacked stone. We are an outdoorsy family, so it looked perfect. We then looked it up on our phones, got the directions, and pressed go. After we fought traffic for almost 10 minutes, we realized the blinking blue dot on our map app took us in a complete square to the back of the same building in front of which we had just parked. It would have been much quicker to walk. The story gets better. So, we walk up to this National Park-like lodge restaurant, and it appeared on the *outside* as advertised. However, what we didn't notice at first on the *inside* was that there were no other children, families, or even couples. We began to notice that all the patrons were male and all the wait staff female. Imagine our surprise, when it all came together for us, sitting there as a precious young family after church.

Technology is a tool to help us plan, but never the plan itself. And that plan must include accurate information about the destination—how to get there and what it really is!

We don't plan for the sake of planning. We plan so that things go well and so that things go quicker.

Our plan doesn't have to be written down, but we must think through potential consequences of our actions. That said, this lifelong learning of leadership is indeed an adaptive process—we learn as we go. It is a marathon, not a sprint, and one with no finish line. Within the course of that race, let's start with some stretches and stay flexible, because...

SOME THINGS WE JUST CAN'T PLAN

I was 5 years old at a campground in Maine, when my dear mother entered me in a bubblegum blowing contest. The problem was mom never let us chew gum as kids. Fortunately, in a line with other children across the front of a make-shift stage, I didn't have to walk and chew gum at the same time. But how to *blow* a bubble? There are some things we just can't plan. I guess dear mother thought that would be funny (in addition to being voted Most Athletic her senior year in high school, my wild mother was also voted Class Clown). Though not quite an athletic event, I wanted to succeed and impress mom, so I planned to deliver a bubble to the cheering crowd no matter what it took. I poked my tongue out. Spittle flew. Then a tight ball of gum dropped between my shoes, and that was my third attempt. It was quite

166

the scene, the bubble never came, and I've been scarred ever since. You think that's bad?

My wife Lulie had a live opossum land on her head. A student at Louisiana State University in Baton Rouge, she worked evenings as a waitress. One night as Lulie's shift ended, she exited the employee door of Mike Anderson's Seafood Restaurant. Lulie felt what she thought was a brick hit her head. The opossum may have had greasy feet and slipped off the roof, or perhaps he chose to engage with Lulie for purely social reasons. However, Lulie was in no mood to play, and she certainly wasn't about to play possum. Quick as a frog off a lily pad, Lulie sprang to her car. She jammed the stick shift in reverse and screeched out of the parking lot, unsure exactly who did what but pretty certain a brick was thrown at her head. Only later did Lulie learn what happened, and then most of Baton Rouge knew too. The event was covered in the news, courtesy of her boss as the eyewitness who called the incident in to his contact at the local paper. I want to quickly add that another opossum made headlines in that same town two decades later in 2016, running onto the Louisiana State University baseball field during a game. Following that escapade, LSU went on a run of impressive victories, especially during late-game rallies. So memorable was that string of victories—and the opossum that started it all—that a Cajun country singer and lifelong LSU baseball fan recorded a music video tribute entitled, "Fear the Possum."

There are some things we just can't plan for. How we respond, though—learn from and grow from—such events in life outlines our path ahead.

Back to the opossum on my wife's head. You'd have to know my wife. She is the most humble and selfless person I know; in more than a quarter century of marriage I've never heard Lulie brag even once, and, unlike the opossum, she has never sought the limelight. So, how did she deal with the opossum incident? Lulie's options were four-

167

fold: *hit back* and call the local Animal Damage Control office; avoid others and their questions (the *play dead* approach); simply *brush off* or minimize the event; or *embrace* the story. Lulie chose the latter and dealt with it *head-on* (Again, I could not resist). As a result, Lulie addressed all questions with good humor, the masses were satisfied, and interest waned. There was no hint at a cover-up, so no additional story to cover, at least not with Lulie as the central figure. Opossums in Baton Rouge have gone on to fame, and my wife to good fortune. There are some things we just can't plan. So, when we can…

KNOW WHAT WE'RE GETTING INTO

Three short stories follow from my youth coaching, and time in the field as a wildlife biologist. I call them Putt-Putt, The Explosion, and Thermometer. Hopefully they help highlight the importance of leaders' proper preparation.

Putt-Putt

As a lad I loved putt-putt or miniature golf. I had no reason to believe I was any good at it—no data to support my theory that I was amazing—but I did anyway. So, I and Tony Ruccione, my best friend in middle school, scrounged up entrance fee funds and convinced his dad to drive us quite a way to the nearest tournament. Tony and I, paired throughout the 18-hole course, were quite the pair indeed, high-fiving with each putt landing true, absorbed in our own play, and unaware of the performance of those around us. We were in the midst of our own battle. Tony led, then I led, and vice-versa; in the end, we tied. Our overall finish was tied for 11th place. "Yes! Almost top 10!" I exclaimed. We later learned there were 12 participants in the tournament. Only as the results were read did I look around at the competition. I didn't know it was a thing to coordinate the colors of one's putt-putt ball, golf club, and golf outfit. A light went on for me, and I thought of the Shel Silverstein poem from a *A Light in the Attic*:

They said come skating;

They said it's so nice.

They said coming skating;

I'd done it twice.

They said come skating;

It sounded nice...

I wore roller—

They meant ice. [65]

The Explosion

Of the five sports I coached, I thought I was best at coaching basketball. With the best of intentions, I brought my unbridled, irrational optimism into coaching my fourth season of youth basketball. After a great sales pitch to parents on a team vision—and oblivious to the ominous foreshadowing—I chose the name *The Explosion*. I took my son, several of his friends, and a half dozen other better 4th-grade players from typical recreational league basketball to travel to play more elite competition. Game one matched us against who I thought was the weakest team in the travel league. Mind you, I had no data to support that supposition. If you judged them by their final record that year, it was evident that they were terrible. It's just that we were worse. They blew us out of the gym that first game on our way to a 0-13 record. Though the team was *The Explosion*, from the start their coach's lack of preparation created an implosion.

Thermometer

Up ahead on the trail, the lead wildlife research saw movement, and we all heard a loud snort. "We got one!" he exclaimed. My heart beats out-paced my boot steps as we closed the gap between us three and the supposed captured Louisiana black bear, then on the federal list of endangered species. Since it was my first time in the field to study bears, I felt a sense of danger in that deep, dark, closed-canopy woods called a bottomland hardwood, with little sunlight penetrating the forest floor. As we approached the massive bear, restrained by just one relatively soft leg-hold trap, I became anxious. My thoughts were not that this subspecies had a role in the creation of the cute "Teddy Bear," which followed the media's coverage of President Teddy Roosevelt's refusal to shoot a Louisiana black bear on a hunt near where I was standing almost a century before. Instead, my mind was on the question: what if our shot with the tranquilizer dart did not land true? Would I experience first-hand what science knew but popular culture did not? The lion, though dubbed king of beasts, is no match for the more powerful North American bear species. My question could wait for another day, fortunately, as our tranquilizer dart landed on target and the big bear was then fast asleep. Being a rookie with two veterans of bear biology, I stood in awe for several minutes while one affixed the radio collar and the other began to extract blood samples. Hoping to take measurements but grateful to help in any way, I asked what I can do to help once I realized they forgot I was there. The lead said, "take its temperature," and the other pointed to the bag that held the thermometer. Though I still needed one more bit of instruction, I saw them turn back to their time-sensitive work. So, I did the best I could and gently lifted the bear's tongue and softly placed the thermometer under it. Almost in unison, each with a sly smirk, they exclaimed, "Wrong end!" Four years later at my wedding reception—and the bear story well-traveled among my friends and family—my brother and Best Man ensured that the groom's cake, in the shape of a black bear, featured a real thermometer inserted in the correct end.

Sometimes there's no way to know what we're getting into; things just happen. Most of the time, however, we make our leadership and life easier with one more piece of data or well-placed question.

I could have planned and prepared better in all three instances. I should have known more about my putt-putt and basketball competition, and I could have asked how best to place the thermometer. All data simple to uncover. Most of the time planning is easier than we think, and it's quite possible to know what we're getting into. We can take it a step further, and believe it or not, with some certainty...

WE CAN PREDICT THE FUTURE

We *can* predict the future. It's easier than we think, and we don't need to obtain tarot cards or a crystal ball, nor must we light candles, burn incense, or consult the ghostly living or ghastly dead.

When my oldest son, Dane, was just 18 months old he could mimic 18 bird calls. At age four Dane knew there were two dozen species of alligators and crocodiles in the world and could correctly pronounce the names of those in the western hemisphere. I didn't know half that and I spent five years getting a degree in that sort of stuff. So, before I could be asked if I was smarter than a fifth grader, I stopped debating most facts and figures with Dane his third-grade year. More than an ability to regurgitate facts from the past, though, Dane thinks through future scenarios and implements long-term plans. In 8th grade he devised a plan to get into the Georgia Institute of Technology, a top engineering school. Dane scheduled 12 high school advanced placement or "AP" courses through each of eight semesters, all while immersed in numerous extracurricular activities. Dane spent many an otherwise free hour thinking through potential test problems in high school, and, later, Georgia Tech, where he graduated with honors. But there was one summer afternoon Dane had a thought, but not a thoughtful plan. He didn't think past the first step. We were in our driveway, washing our family fleet of three old cars, and Dane thought it would be more convenient to place my tiny Toyota Scion in neutral and push it out of the way, rather than run upstairs and grab the keys. After all, a Scion is so small and light. To this day I'm amazed how quickly an object in motion can gain momentum on the slightest of declines. I am also amazed how a small tree can make such a large dent in a car.

Dane is a quick learner and will likely not repeat that mistake, but I'm surprised how many people, including myself, don't learn lessons sooner. I have witnessed nine out of ten people I know do the same thing over and over and expect a different result—the definition of insanity some say. I say that's the typical person's approach to life. A friend, describing more than twenty thousand dollars of credit card debt amassed, exclaimed, "I don't know how I got into this situation!" Well friend, you spent more than you earned, and for quite some time. Another friend, who too will remain nameless for obvious reasons, said, "I can't believe I gained 45 pounds since college!" I can because I watched you eat more calories than you burned, and for quite some time! (I didn't say that, but I thought it).

Paul George wrote: "Intentions are only as good as the decisions that determine the direction our life goes...If I have the intention of losing weight but never exercise or eat healthy, then my intention accomplishes nothing."[61]

To predict the future, we do two things: study patterns of the past and consider the current path traveled.

To achieve something different, we have to *do* something different. Taylor did, but it wasn't after some...

FALSE STARTS

I love sports, in part because they reflect life itself. Sports provides a view in the mirror to learn more about who we are. We can

172

make observations, work hard, and mark progress. More than just competition, sports offer fun, friendships, fitness, and, above all, life lessons. One life lesson I learned through sports centered on my daughter, Taylor, then 16-years old.

After four years of grueling workouts through middle school and early high school, Taylor clawed her way from a "B-Team" sprinter to her high school track team's "A-Team" in the 4x100 meter sprint relay race. That was, however, until she suffered through two weeks of severe bronchitis which resulted in her losing her coveted place on the team. By mid-season, just in time for the county championship track meet, Taylor's health recovered and her times improved, so the coaches put her on the "B-Team" to show what she could do. As she settled into the starting blocks, the track official held the starter gun in one hand, and with his other clenched a megaphone: "Runners take your mark!" My mind flashed back to 30 minutes before when Taylor "scratched" (or was disqualified) during her third attempt in the long jump event. The relay race was her chance at redemption. The megaphone startled me back to the present: "Get set!" A half-second before the gun blasted, my heart stopped as Taylor leapt forward—disqualified! She took off too soon. All eyes in the stadium were on my daughter as the official escorted her off the track. Taylor looked down for several minutes, and later looked inward for several days. The week ahead would determine her track future and give a glimpse into who she really was.

"Wanna race?" I asked my daughter near the end of her spring break vacation. Exactly seven days earlier she walked off that chilly north Georgia track, disqualified. But that day found her in warm south Florida, on Sanibel Island.

Not everything will go well, so let us anticipate False Starts, and intentionally build time into plans to recover from failure and get back on (the) track!

Taylor exercised every day that week. One day I found her doing sprints in the hotel parking lot in the searing heat. Repetition after repetition, Taylor was perhaps contemplating Andy Stanley's advice: "Your direction not your intention determines your destination." Maybe she was reflecting back before moving forward, thinking of the Kay Lyons quote: "Yesterday is a canceled check; tomorrow is a promissory note; today is the only cash you have—so spend it wisely," which is a version of the Eskimo saying: "Yesterday is ashes; tomorrow wood. Only today does the fire burn brightly." As the sun burned brightly and the red-hot asphalt burned her hands, I doubt Taylor was actually thinking of leadership quotes. I was though, and I recalled the essence of Annie Dillard saying, "How we spend our days is, of course, how we spend our lives."

Taylor agreed to my sprint race challenge with no hesitation, and then blew me away. It wasn't even close. I'd never seen her run so fast, and I'd seen every race of her life. One week before my heart broke for Taylor, but that particular day my heart nearly burst out of my swelled chest. I didn't know how Taylor would do with track that year, but I was certain she would finish strong in life.

Back on the track the next week it took only a matter of days, not even weeks for Taylor to earn back her spot on the A-Team. Her relay team went on to break a decade-old school record that still stands as of the printing of this book.

About a third of the way through this chapter about planning, you may have noticed that so far, we have covered the mindset of planning and not the mechanics. Though we will touch on a few key planning how-tos going forward, we will focus more on the mindset of planning because most organizations have a shelf full of three-ring binders—or an electronic folder full of examples—on the required steps of planning unique to an organization. It is more important to take a fresh, perhaps wild, approach to planning and spend time on the big picture—the why and the what—of planning before one zooms down into the details of the how, who, and when. So, let us recap some key tenets of planning by way of the section titles we have completed: As we plan, let us remember from the outset that there are Some Things We Just Can't Plan, so let us stay flexible. To the best of our ability, though, let us Know What We're Getting Into. That is not as hard as we think because more often than not, We Can Predict the Future. Going forward, let us consider that some plans unfold slowly, but know that it's okay to...

SLOW DOWN TO GO FAST

I often rush to solutions without first contemplating the problem, and when I do slow down to contemplate, I often skip over proper preparation and jump right in. A wild approach to leadership is to slow down to go fast. If we slow down to think deeper and slow down to prepare better, we will ultimately go faster over the long-term.

The children's story about the tortoise and the hare comes to mind as does the adult book *The 7 Habitats of Highly Effective People*. "Seek first to understand" is a memorable phrase from Dr. Steven Covey's landmark leadership book.[21] Dr. Albert Einstein said that "If I had an hour to solve a problem and my life depended on the solution, I would spend the first 55 minutes determining the proper question to ask." Abraham Lincoln said, "If I had eight hours to chop down a tree,

When we move too fast with supposed efficiency, we often lose long-term effectiveness. We often miss the best solution and the healthy sustainability of people, including ourselves.

I'd spend six hours sharpening my ax." A little closer to home for me, I consulted the advice of my brother-in-law, Paul George. No, not the professional basketball player Paul George, but the same-named speaker, author, and executive coach who wrote in his book, *Rethink Happiness*: "I'm guilty of…running at a pace I'm not meant for. I'm guilty of thinking that my fast pace is productive and that my productivity affirms my identity…We are all caught up in a game of life and move at a pace we aren't created for, all the while running over things, even people."[61] We have a spill-over effect on others; our fast pace can not only hinder the best solution, but it also negatively impacts other people. The authors of *Scrum* wrote, "…overworked employees get more distracted and begin distracting others. Soon they're making bad decisions…"[30]

If my mistakes and my brother-in-law's wisdom have not quite convinced you, at least reconsider the advice above from Abe Lincoln and Drs. Covey and Einstein. Seek first to understand, contemplate the problem, and sharpen the ax—whether an external challenge or our internal health. As we slow down to go fast—take short term efficiency loss for a long-term effectiveness gain—that doesn't mean we stall our plans, because…

PATIENCE ISN'T "DO NOTHING"

We have all heard someone tell us, with good intention, "Have patience." However, we never hear the rest of what good advice could be if only the following words were added: "But while you wait, how about…" What if a medical doctor's strategy with her patient was always, "We're just going wait this thing out and see what happens." Point being, there is always something we can be doing while we wait, to make the most of our time before what's to come.

In *An Enemy Called Average*, John L. Mason writes about patience and planning in the growing of bamboo in the Far East:

"During the first four years they water and fertilize the plant with seemingly little or no results. Then the fifth year they again

176

apply water and fertilizer—and in five weeks' time the tree grows to ninety feet in height! The obvious question is: did the Chinese bamboo tree grow ninety feet in five weeks, or did it grow ninety feet in five years? The answer is: it grew ninety feet in five years. Because if at any time during those five years the people had stopped watering and fertilizing the tree, it would have died."[52]

In the story of my daughter Taylor on the track in the last section, did she win back her A-Team position by doing sprints in the hotel parking lot, or did Taylor earn back her slot by first spending four years building a firm foundation for fitness? The answer is that she needed to do both to put herself into a position to be successful.

After we set our planning goal, consider our unique role *in between* the milestones and deadlines.

Whether you listen to the rap lyrics of Whodini—"But in the meantime, the in between time...*if you work your thing, then I'll work mine*"—or if you hear the rural lyrics of Montgomery Gentry's voice— "Put me 'round a campfire cookin' something I just cleaned...*you do your thing, and I'll do mine*"—the key is to ask ourselves what is it that we alone can do in the in between time? Do we have a...

- ...goal to read 25 books in 25 weeks? Listen to audiobooks on the Interstate.
- ...speech to give in two weeks? Make note cards day 1 and practice on the dog day 2.
- ...room to organize by Friday—and it's a wreck? What three things can I pick up now?
- ...surprise meet and greet with new the CEO this afternoon? Google her at lunch.

- ...twelve-chapter book due in a year? Draft chapter one by January 31.
- ...15-minute wait before relay teammates arrive? Sit quiet and visualize your handoff.

Examples are endless. In both the development and implementation of a plan, patience isn't "do nothing." There is always something we alone or as part of a team we can do to move a plan to reality. Sometimes during that time a well-placed question should be pondered, like...

DO YOU HAVE A WIG?

A wild approach to leadership is to make sure we have wigs and the right number of them. Their color, texture, length, and style are less important than the number.

Often spoken and written as the acronym WIG, our Wildly Important Goals do not have to be complex or barely attainable. It's just that WIGs are activities so wildly important that they must be done as a top priority—or the only priority. In *Accelerate: Building Strategic Agility for a Faster-Moving World*, John P. Kotter says to, "Create a sense of urgency around a single big opportunity."[19] For the United States' space program in the early 1960s, did President John F. Kennedy say, "These are the 17 things we will do to strength our outer space capabilities?" No, JFK, known for his great hair, also had a WIG and said, "before this decade is out," we will rally around, "...landing a man on the moon and returning him safely to the earth." It was one planning goal to focus on that included who will do what by when. Wildly important goals are a focus for other activities to fall under, provided they support the ultimate goal. Five-time college basketball national champion coach Mike Krzyzewski further advised us that, "Goals should be realistic, attainable, and shared among all members of the team."

If you are like me and struggle to settle on one planning goal, pick two or three at the most, says the research.

The authors of *The 4 Disciplines of Execution: Achieving Your Wildly Important Goals* caution us, however, against having too many goals. They said at a point we will see diminishing returns with too many goals: when you set just to two or three goals you most often get two or three done. When you set four to ten goals you get only one or two done. When you set 11-20 goals, the most common result is no goals get completed.[10]

While it is essential to focus, plans are strongest when we first...

GATHER ROCK SOLID INPUT

The United States Army Corps of Engineers and the U.S. Department of the Interior were not close partners on environmental issues historically, but, in south Florida's Everglades, Rock Salt brought them a lot closer together. Rock Salt was not a mineral, rather a gem—no, a jewel.

Minerals occur naturally in the crust of the earth and are inorganic solids. Not too impressive. A gem, however, is a piece of mineral, which, when cut and polished, makes for jewelry. Terrence C. "Rock" Salt—with conservation's coolest first and last name combination—was a jewel in the crown of achievement of Everglades restoration. A West Point graduate and retired colonel, Rock Salt must have recalled from his master's degree in physics that a property of matter continues in its existing state of rest or consistent motion unless that state is changed by an external force. He was so well respected that two organizations, historically on opposite sides of the negotiating table, took turns hiring him as a leader. For two decades he worked for the Army Corps of Engineers, then the Department of the Interior, and then the Army Corps of Engineers again. Working for the Corps *and* Interior, Rock helped ensure the *and*—not an *or*—in the delicate Everglades balance of water for people *and* water for wildlife. How did he do it?

While working on his master's in physics, Rock Salt may have taken a history lesson and considered the words of Thomas Jefferson: "In matters of style, swim with the current; in matters of principle, stand like a rock." The rock in Rock Salt stood firm in matters of character and integrity. In matters of style, the salt in Rock Salt would dissolve and go with the flow or swim with the current. Because of that, he was both trusted and liked. He leveraged that goodwill when he gathered input.

Input makes our final products stronger as we include others' ideas and ensure their ownership—a buy-in best ensured by a meaningful be-in. Let us have key people be in the process early and often.

In a wild approach to leadership to gathering input, Rock Salt would share conflicting opinions or negative perspectives in draft letters ahead of time with the opposing side. He did this because he wanted:

(a) there to be no surprises to maintain trust;

(b) an opportunity to get other's thoughts to ensure he had the right information and got the information right; and

(c) to provide others a chance to change their position or fix whatever was the problem.

Rock's goal was that the final, official correspondence on the matter would have a different tone at minimum, if not entirely different content. Rock's preferred final letter was a thank you letter with the issue informally resolved before it was formally addressed.

Input, the putting in of the new, is a life-giving effort. We must plan for the new and the different. We don't have to. We do have a choice. It is...

CHANGE OR DIE

Before we end the chapter on a high note, let us consider this wild approach to leadership: change or die. Change or die is an approach in which I find life, joy, and hope. It's because if we want to live as an individual, team, or organization, we must plan to be flexible and adapt.

There's an old saying: "The more things change, the more they stay the same." That's very catchy. Just one problem: it doesn't make any sense.

My youngest son, Matthew, in third grade at the time, asked, "Daddy, do all animals have adaptations?" I thought for a moment then answered, "Yes. Any species that didn't adapt over time wouldn't be here. It would be extinct". The same is true for organizations, and I dare say individuals. Don't just take my word for it, however. Robert Kegan and Lisa Laskow Lahey write in *Immunity to Change*: "Change or die. That's the choice that doctors give at-risk heart patients, (but) only one is seven is able to make the necessary life-style changes. Even when it's a matter of life or death, the ability to change remains the greatest challenge for most individuals."[34] The authors of *Switch* explain why people don't make the switch: "Change is hard because people are reluctant to alter habits that have been successful in the past"[32]

Dee Hock, founder and former Chief Executive Officer of VISA, said that we, "...learn nothing from your success except to think too much of yourself. It is from failure that all growth comes, provided you can recognize it, admit it, learn from it ... and then try again." I disagree with Hock that all growth comes from failure, as we can grow

181

by learning from others' successes and our own. Our challenge indeed is not to get complacent in our success. Indeed, change or die. And if we experience setback along the way, we can tell ourselves...

I GET KNOCKED DOWN, BUT I GET UP AGAIN

Let me tell you first, though, about the time I just swayed.

I was the new kid in 6th grade. Few kids were nice to me in the deep south as I had a strange accent from up north. Frank J. Edmondson was nice to me though. I initially thought so because we were both different; I the only New York transplant, and he one of just five African American boys in our class of sixty. I learned over time, though, that Frank was kind to me because he's just kind. That was a rare trait indeed in early middle school. Fast-forward fifteen years and Frank was a groomsman in my wedding. But let's fast-forward just ten years after we met when his elderly aunt died. I arrived a couple minutes late to her funeral. I made my way through the crowd which spilled out the small country church door. I wanted Frank to see that I made it. I would be easy to spot as the only European American out of nearly a hundred African American mourners. From behind the casket, Frank, literally the best singer I know, swayed with the choir. He saw me and waved me over. I didn't know where I would sit, as every seat was full, but I trusted that he saw a spot for me up front. As I made my way down the left side of the church toward him—and while he sang and held his left hand high in unison with the swaying choir—Frank gestured with his right hand for me to sit in the nook at the far side of the choir against the wall. So there I was smashed between the wall and the choir, but real close to the front row in a spot I *thought* I could remain unseen. However, the very stout woman between Frank and I elbowed me hard and motioned to stand up. She gave me a look I'd only seen in my disappointed mother and grandmother, but in a matter of moments her frown turned upside down as I stood, sang, clapped, and swayed. For that one afternoon, I had joined the gospel choir. If you've heard me sing, however, you would have expected Frank's aunt to roll over in her casket.

As we close out this chapter on planning, let us remember that sometimes the best laid plans changes, and sometimes we don't even know what we're getting into. Sometimes we roll with the punches, and sometimes sway with the choir. Sometimes we get knocked down. The key is to get up again.

While you may not know the British band *Chumbawamba* nor likely recall the title of their 1997 hit song *Tubthumping* (which doesn't appear to have anything to do with the words of the song), I'm certain you would not forget the song's melody or main lyrics—repeated more than two dozen times in about three minutes: *I get knocked down, but I get up again. You are never gonna keep me down.* That song came out the year my oldest, Dane, was born. I don't know if the words inspired his mother and I through 3:00 a.m. feedings, or if it was Dane's anthem while he learned to walk. *I get knocked down, but I get up again. You are never gonna keep me down.* However, if you have heard this song before, chances are you are singing them in your head right now. The tune is catchy and the phrase memorable. That tune may stay with you the rest of today and into tomorrow, be forewarned. These words, though, can help us all going forward. Let us break them down into their three parts: an external challenge, an internal choice, and a commitment.

I get knocked down…an external challenge
But I get up again…an internal choice
You are never gonna keep me down…a commitment.

Are you unsure if you want to take advice from a band called *Chumbawamba* in a song titled *Tubthumping?* Alright then, let's consult others, starting with writer F. Scott Fitzgerald, who said, "Never confuse a single defeat with a final defeat." Few may know more about victory than professional basketball's five-time most valuable player and six-time world champion, Michael Jordan. But MJ said: "I've missed more than 9,000 shots in my career. I've lost almost 300 games. Twenty-six times I've been trusted to take the game winning shot and missed. I've failed over and over and over again in my life. And that is why I succeed." Why he and other greats succeed is that they learn from mistakes. Learning from mistakes is to not repeat the same mistakes. Tony Sutherland writes in *Leader Slips* that "Failure is not a title, it's an event. Failure doesn't have to be fatal or final. In fact, failure can be fruitful if we learn from it." Sutherland writes that learning from our mistakes teaches us to sharpen our focus, align our aim at the target, stretch the arrow back, and shoot again.

A key question: what are we shooting towards or aiming for? This is indeed the most important consideration, so we conclude this book with...

CHAPTER 8

Priorities — Focus On Essential

INTRODUCTION

The two chapters you just read, Policy and Planning, had strong themes of efficiency. This last chapter emphasizes effectiveness—a focus on priorities. The author of *Principle-Centered Leadership* wrote that, "Effective people lead their lives and manage their relationships around principles; ineffective people attempt to manage their time around priorities and their tasks around goals. Think effectiveness with people; efficiency with things." We will unpack that and more as we move through these final ten sections of our last chapter.

We begin with a reminder to *Lead With The Why* and then to not make things harder than they have to be. This is because leadership and life are a *Simple Race, Not a Steeplechase* after all. But exactly how do we keep life a Simple Race? We compare what we think we must do against the *5-D Filter*. After that instruction and before closing inspiration, we are reminded of the *Multi-tasking Myth* and how important it is to *Deal in Hope*. We close with matters of faith, life, death, and the concept of time itself with sections titled *Netflix With*

God, A Wonderful Life, Live Like You're Dying, It's about T-I-M-E, and *And It's About Time!* Let's start in the right place. Let's...

LEAD WITH THE WHY

Let's pretend I am your middle school English teacher. "Class, as I write four words in a row, quickly as you can, say out loud what the next two are. Ready? Here we go: 'Who, what, when, where, (____), and (____).'"

I will guess that before I even finished writing the first four words you knew that the last two words would be why and how. Those six words and in that order have been drilled into most of our heads. However, I am not an English teacher and you're probably not either. Well, maybe a couple of you are. We are all leaders or can be, and leaders don't order things as to who, what, when, where, why, and how. We're not teaching a class or writing a paper; we are connecting with and leading people.

A leader leads with the why for the who.

Let's go back in time well before middle school. If you were once a baby, there's a good chance your first words were some versions of ma-ma or da-da. You then learned the word no. Later, however, as a young child, you learned another—not who, what, when, where, or how. But why. From the young child to the mature adult, we all crave the why. Let us never forget that the individuals and teams we lead are no different. Everyone wants to know the reason or purpose—behind a project, a priority, and even life itself.

Do you lead with they why or manage with how? Simon Sinek, author of *Start With Why* was made famous for his TED Talk which has been viewed tens of millions of times. Sinek said there is a difference between giving *direction* and giving *directions*. Steve Coughran, author and Chief Financial Officer of an international billion-dollar company, says that the most influential bosses leave the how to their employees to figure out. He says that poor leaders provide specificity around how to complete a task but fail to share the big picture—the why—behind the request.

So let's summarize our role as leaders relative to the six words we keep repeating here. Leaders focus on purpose (why) and select and develop people (who). Leaders streamline policy (what) and sometimes set deadlines (when). Leaders try to avoid detailed instruction (how) and location (where). A wild approach to leadership is to go beyond just *start with why*, and instead *lead with the why*. *Lead* rather than *start* implies they we do it continuously, not once. Lead with the why reminds us to focus on and communicate the most compelling purpose of our work …and our very being—what we wanted to know as a young child and what we all crave still today. But before we get too deep, let us try to keep things simple and remember life and work often is a…

SIMPLE RACE, NOT A STEEPLE CHASE

My sports rival in 8th grade, Tim Hoosier, made an unnecessary steeple chase out of a simple race. He didn't have to take the challenging route over obstacles, but he did anyway. Tim was a large-framed 6'5" runner for a rival school. A basketball player, he signed up for cross country to improve his endurance and strengthen his legs to avoid injuries. Given that, it was most curious then that Tim chose the path he did during an otherwise straightforward three-mile cross country race. The only thing he had to do was run a clearly marked one-mile course three times, but as we neared the one-third mark a group of girls cheered his name. Though I heard them yell, "Go Tim," he must have heard "You can fly" because he then tried to soar over a chain strung two feet high between two posts. Tim's back foot caught the chain, and he swung forward, face-first, with an audible thump to the ground. There was blood on his face but Tim kept going. Another mile later the girls were cheering again as he approached the chain. His toe did not catch the chain this time, but his shin did. "Thud!" More blood. One mile later and the race almost done, Time summoned every bit of energy he had left. With clenched fists he sprinted toward the chain, the girls cheered, and he jumped higher than his last attempt...but not as high as his first. "Thud!" More blood. I both pitied and admired Tim as he got up a third time then finished the race. I told this story to my oldest son with the intention to make a big life lesson out of it: avoid obstacles and never give up. However, before I could get to the punch line, Dane interjected: "If you saw Tim fall two times and were still behind him to watch a third spill, you must have been really slow."

I hadn't thought about that until then. Thanks, Dane. It was no tortoise and the hare lesson. Indeed, I started, stayed, and finished behind Tim. I got a great story out of it, though: Tim didn't have to do what he convinced himself he had to in order to impress others. It was a simple race, Tim, not a steeplechase.

We often put unnecessary obstacles in our way and make things harder than they have to be.

Let's not do that. Leadership is hard enough, so here's new help: before we decide to run with something, run it through the...

5-D FILTER

The best way to say yes to what's most important is to say no to lower priorities. We create the most time for the best things not when we neatly order our top five priorities, but when we say no to the lower five or approach them differently. What we do most often, however, is agree to something first, *then later think* of the impact to our workload and the workload of those we lead. That is, *if we give it any thought at all.*

There is another way. The 5-D filter is a memorable set of options to manage workload.

Ask before a task, can I:
> Delete?
> Do Differently?
> Delay?
> Delegate?
> Do?

The most critical part of our work week and workday is before we actually start anything—the first 15 minutes or more before we receive our first visitor, check our texts, open our email, scroll through social media, or see what's in your hard copy inbox (for those of us who still have them). This is when it is most important that we run things through the 5-D filter. We can use the filter not only each day, but before each task—or before each month, quarter, or year. The time scale matters not as much as actually asking the questions: what can be *deleted* all together, what can be done *differently*, what can we *delay* for a better time, what can be delegated to someone else, and then what must I or we *do*? The latter includes what is it that only I can *do* and have to *do*.

Each of the 5-D filter steps are covered below in a little more detail. They are most impactful implemented in the order below.

1. **Delete**

Saying no to something—deleting it off the list—is the hardest part of workload management, but it is where the best work of leaders is done. This is the hardest step because we care so much about all of our work and the many possibilities. It's easy to come up with a new list of top three or top ten priorities. This is what some leaders do, and then they pat themselves on the back afterwards. Those of us down the food chain know the painful truth: all they are doing is either adding more work to the do-list or rearranging the order of things that we'd be doing anyway. The best way—and often the only way—to say yes to what's most important is to say no to lower priorities. That is how we actually free up time to focus more on what's most important.

2. **Do differently**

When an adult told us to eat what was on our plate, didn't that usually mean all of it? The answer is also yes to mow all of the lawn, complete every answer on a test, and brush each and every tooth. What we were trained to do at home and school, however, is the exact opposite of the mindset we must have at work to survive the e-mail and inbox barrage. A wild approach to leadership is to focus more on what not to do and to take shortcuts whenever and wherever you can. Paraphrasing 1700's French writer, philosopher, and historian, Voltaire: Don't let the perfect be the enemy of the good. Said another way this century by Sheryl Sandberg: "Done is better than perfect." Some work must be A+ because it's for the CEO, it's going to mass print, or it's what we take into the courtroom with our lawyer to the see the judge. However, for everything else, consider if C+ or a solid B would do just fine.

3. **Delay**

Few things at work are as arbitrary as the deadline. We make things due for ourselves and others at "close of business," "by the end of the week," or "at month's end" as if those phrases will be momentous occasions with eternal significance. They're not. They're usually arbitrary, and we often have a lot of control when they are set. If someone else sets the deadline, more often than not if we ask, "Would it be okay if I took three more days to complete it?" the answer is almost always, "oh, sure." Why delay some things? Like when we delete things, it allows more focus right now on what's most important.

4. **Delegate**

When we delegate, consider that while we delete something from our work list, we add it to another's. Therefore, delegation shouldn't be a simple solution or done lightly. When a leader assigns something, the follower often feels that the action has greater significance than other items on their list, even if the task isn't more important than anything else (Let us remember that our staff forgets we are not any smarter than they are). The best questions for a leader to ask are: "what is it that only I can do, and no one else?" We are advised by author and leader Andy Stanley to not give up what is unique to us—to do only that we can do.

5. **Do**

We arrive at this step 5 only after we consider steps 1-4. Okay, so now we decided to do the thing. What now? You'll love this: now see if parts of the task can be deleted, done differently, delayed, or delegated. Why spend so much time with the 5-D filter? Our time is our most precious resource. When it's gone, it's gone—forever. Steve Jobs of Apple once said that, "People think focus means saying yes to the thing you've got to focus on. But that's not what it means at all. It means saying no to the hundred other good ideas that there are. You have to pick carefully." After we pick carefully that which only we can do, let us not fool ourselves that we can juggle a couple other things well at the same time. That is the...

MULTI-TASKING MYTH

I try to get each and every two-handled plastic grocery bag from the back of the car up to the kitchen in one trip *to save time*.

However, it's never one of the six bags I have my two arms through that tear. It's one of the eight more I have precariously twisted around each my fingers that slips off, and the bag's contents usually takes a tumble down the stairs. The time I spend picking up the spaghetti boxes, taco seasoning packets, cans of Rotel tomatoes, and rolls of paper towels that just kept rolling, makes me wonder if two trips with half the bags might have been quicker.

I continue to try to prove effective multi-tasking is possible, but I'm the guy who struggles to walk and chew gum. Definitely don't ask me to blow bubbles as well. I kid you not, the afternoon before I wrote this section I was on the phone with Holly, and I called her Harry, because that was the name I just read in the email as I talked to her.

Oh sure, we can do two things at once, but neither one is done very well. Effective multi-tasking is a myth.

After we consult the 5-D filter and decide to do something, let's do it well. Consider that research shows *quantitatively* that our minds can only effectively address and remember well one thing at a time, and great coaches will tell us *qualitatively* that we are happier and more relaxed when we are focused on one-thing in the moment. Phil Jackson, 11-time professional basketball world champion coach said, "...true joy comes from being fully present in each and every moment, not just when things are going your way. Of course, it's no accident that things are more likely to go your way when you...focus your full attention on what's happening *right this moment*." The college football coach with the most national championships of all time, Nick Saban, said: "What happened yesterday is history. What happens tomorrow is a mystery. What we do today makes a difference—the precious present moment."[26] If we must multi-task with things now and then, so be it. But let us stay present with precious people, and never lose focus on others in need. It is most essential as a leader that we...

192

DEAL IN HOPE

We now make the final pivot in *Wild Approach Leadership* in this essential chapter about priorities. We now focus completely on our relationships with people. Much help comes from hope. An array of leaders, each in their own way, communicated the power of hope. Infamous dictator Napoleon Bonaparte of France recognizing the tremendous rallying power of a positive, forward-thinking vision, said explicitly that, "a leader is a dealer in hope." Former United States President Ronald Reagan's sunny optimism warmed even some of his coldest policy critics. The movie about kind and upbeat Mr. Rogers, *A Beautiful Day in the Neighborhood,* made $15 million on opening weekend.

What united those three very unique leaders was not so much their unbridled optimism, but the hope they maintained while also confronting challenges. A sustainable, believable hope for a brighter future is best communicated not through rose-colored glasses, but instead through the glass half full versus half empty metaphor. You've likely heard it said that optimists believe the proverbial glass is half full, and the pessimists believe the glass is half empty. Who is right? They both are. I say only slightly tongue-in-cheek that a wild approach to leadership is to stand with a firm leg on each side of the great divide of that raging debate and regularly, publicly declare that the glass can indeed be half empty and also half full.

We are best served—and at our best to serve others—when we acknowledge both the negative and positive as leaders. We then harness the positive attributes of a situation to help navigate.

That does not mean, however, that as we confront the negatives—the brutal realities in some situations—that we share those challenges with a pessimistic attitude. In *Ride of Lifetime*, Bob Igor, then leader of The Walt Disney Company and its more than 200,000 employees said that there are, "...plenty of valid reasons to be pessimistic, but as a leader you can't communicate that pessimism to the people around you...It saps energy and inspiration...Optimism sets a different machine in motion...This isn't about saying things are good when they're not, and it's not about conveying some innate faith that 'things will work out.' It's about believing you and the people around you can steer toward the best outcome..."[73] Let's get real next, but through our imagination, moving from Disney to...

NETFLIX WITH GOD

In the 2013 movie, *About Time,* the lead character said: "I just try to live every day as if I've deliberately come back to this one day, to enjoy it, as if it was the full final day of my extraordinary, ordinary life." That would be an *enjoyable* life, but if we want a more meaningful, impactful life of *giving joy* to others, consider the following wild approach to leadership. Imagine at the conclusion of our life we have a date to watch Netflix with God, and the true story film details our life. It's called *What if I Knew?* My Netflix with God would include a haunting scene with the most tragic of consequences. God would say to me, "Do you see that lady beside you on the plane? No, not that one. The one on the other side of you who appeared to have it all together. You did not take out your earbud on that side of your head to hear her say hello and offer a kind word in return. That was all she was looking for, not so much in that moment but in life. Now watch how, a few hours later, you nod a distant, indifferent farewell, not even making eye contact, as she makes her way down the aisle and off the plane. You decided that your music was more important than that person that day. She died by suicide that same night. She asked the heavens that morning for a sign that just one person cared.

Did that event actually happen in my life? Maybe. It could have. Our positive impact on others is hard to quantify, but we can qualify it as...

A WONDERFUL LIFE

The two movies that impacted my life the most could not be more different, or so they would seem on the surface: *It's a Wonderful Life* and *Schindler's List*—one a timeless family favorite, the other a painfully raw Holocaust story. George Bailey sacrificed his career dream, but in doing so improved the lives of an entire town. Oskar Schindler risked his family fortune, and saved more than 1,200 lives. These two films illustrate how measurably important every life and each day is, and both emphasize what would happen if either we had never lived or if we didn't take certain actions.

Here's a wild approach: use death as a motivating life force for yourself, whether to prompt action for a few hours or for a lifetime. Perhaps you struggle like me to spend your time on what matters most in life. For me, it's my precious family, often literally right in front of me, who I retreat from because of the tug of the dirty dishes and unfolded clothes. I have overcome that draw and have spent the most amazing hours with them by telling myself I may die in six hours. We almost never really know when we will die, do we? I ask myself how I want to spend those last few hours on earth. It's never to check one more thing off the to-do list. It is always to draw close with the people who matter most. Granted, this wild approach of shaking our foundation can't be done every day or we'd walk around naked and hungry. We all have work that must be attended to. However, we must not neglect the most precious gifts around us.

Question: Have you ever wondered what people will say about you when you're dead?

Answer: They will say the exact same things they say about you right now when you're not around.

We *can* change both of those conversations, and we can begin right now. Paraphrasing Mahatma Gandhi: be the change you want to see. Begin today to treat others in a way that when we are absent or gone forever, they reflect positively on our impact. Clay Scoggins advises that, "Great leaders look ahead to the future and begin to act today to become who they want to be." [63] Rather than just *think* differently, let's boss ourselves around here. On an app in our phone or on an old-fashioned piece of paper, let us *write down* what we want people to say about us and then live it. Literally write our own eulogy. Write what you want a friend or loved to say one day as they stand at the podium above your coffin. Write those words down, live them, and they will come to life. Until then …

LIVE LIKE YOU'RE DYING

I call on a diverse array of people—Tozer, Tim and Tim, and others—to help me convince you to live now like you're dying. A.W. Tozer who wrote that, "There can be no doubt that this possessive clinging to things is one of the most harmful habits in the life."[60]

If you are reading this book that means you are still alive and it's not too late to cling less to material things and connect more to people and experiences.

Consider the advice of writer Tim Nichols in the Tim McGraw song *Live Like You Were Dying*:

I went skydiving
I went Rocky Mountain climbing
I went 2.7 seconds on a bull named Fumanchu
And I loved deeper
And I spoke sweeter
And I gave forgiveness I'd been denying

***

I was finally the husband
That most of the time I wasn't
And I became a friend a friend would like to have
And all of a sudden going fishin'
Wasn't such an imposition
And I went three times that year I lost my dad

**

Someday I hope you get the chance
To live like you were dying

If Tozer and the Tims haven't convinced you, take the advice of poet Ralph Waldo Emerson: "When you were born you were crying and everyone else was smiling. Live your life so at the end, you're the one who is smiling and everyone else is crying." Why? Because...

IT'S ABOUT T-I-M-E ...

How do you spell love? We don't spell it with letters or even say it most effectively with words. We say it, spell it, and show it when we spend T-I-M-E. Speaker and author Paul George was counseled that his calendar would show what he loved.[61] Actions speak louder than words, never more so than with demonstrating what is really most important to you. President Joe Biden would quote his father: "Don't tell me what your priorities are. Show me your calendar...and I'll tell you what your priorities are."

When I get this right with my youngest son, he misbehaves less often to get attention. When I get this right with my adult children, they open up more and share what matters most to them. When I get this right with my wife, well, that will be the title of my next book, *"Why Was I Such An Idiot for So Long?"*

Actions speak louder than words even with the purest of intentions. I had an excellent boss who was a wonderful human being. He loved his family, asked about everyone else's family, and emphasized the need to prioritize those closest to us by not work too late. However, he worked late almost every day. Can you guess what I and the rest of the staff did? You are right: we worked late almost every day. Why? It's not what the boss said that we listened to, it's what the boss did that we followed. Actions speak louder than words.

Time is never the problem. Heck, it's not even part of the equation; time is set. There's no way to add to it or take it away. It is what it is. No matter where you are, there are still 60 minutes in an hour and 24 hours in a day. Now, exactly how we *choose* to spend our time—what we make priority—is the issue. When she says I didn't have time to get the report done; when he says I didn't have time to fold the clothes; and when she says I didn't have time to practice piano, what they are all *really* saying with their actions is that they didn't make those things a priority. We get further instruction from John Piper, author of the aptly named book, *Don't Waste Your Life*:

> "If you want your life to count, if you want the ripple effect of the pebbles you drop to become waves that reach the end of the earth and roll on into eternity, you don't need to have a high IQ. You don't have to have good looks or riches or come from a fine family or a fine school. Instead, you have to know a few great, majestic, unchanging, obvious, simple, glorious things—or one great all-embracing thing—and be set on fire by them."[6]

To those most important to us at work, and, especially, at home, let us give our time freely.

Nothing says *you are important* more than when we give another our T-I-M-E, one of the few resources that is impossible to replace.

Our most important asset is our time. We can't make any more of it, and when it's gone, it's gone. So, we must guard it carefully. Have some regrets? I do. We cannot change the past, but we can change our future...

AND IT'S ... *ABOUT TIME!*

Frodo said at a difficult juncture in *The Fellowship of the Ring*: "I wish none of this had happened." Gandolf replied: "So do all who live to see such times, but that is not for them to decide. All you have to decide is what to do with the time that is given to you."

Let's decide to spring forward from a strong foundation of connection, character, collaboration, and communication, and express it with people—through good planning and policy—toward our priorities. Is it too late to start?

An ancient Chinese proverb says that the best time to plant a tree was 20 years ago. The second best time is now. Regret for what we *should* have done may be our biggest obstacle to living the life we *can* with joyful purpose. Bob Goff wrote, "We all encounter difficulties. It's what we do next that defines us."

Obstacles from our past won't stop our forward progress unless we carry them along and place them back in front of us.

So, let us take our first step. Spend precious time with the most important people in our life. Write down where we want to be in our journey ahead and write it in the form of a eulogy we want said about us one day. We don't have to do more than that at first. But after that one step, the next one is much easier, because we have begun a journey and we now know which way to go.

199

Acknowledgements

BOOK THANKS...

Thank you, author Tony Sutherland, for being the first to suggest I write a book...and thank you to the whole Sutherland clan for life-long friendships.

Thank you, Author Madelyn Edwards, for the most helpful writing advice.

Thank you to my OG editors: Brenda Fabian, Mark Musaus, Dane Viker, Erik Viker, and Taylor Viker. You made it much better.

Thank you to the personable and professional Publify Publishing team of Sasha, Mimie, and Peter.

Thank you to all the people named in this book. I learned from you during this wild ride.

Thank you, Hamilton Winters, for the connections and advice.

Thank you, Morgan Moore, for risking your camera breaking.

LIFE THANKS ...or there would be no book

Coach Kelly Beckham and Coach Phillip Knight for what you meant to me and hundreds of other young people during our teen years.

The Barr, Keaton, and Akins families for encouraging and welcoming me and teaching me what extended functional families look like who serve their communities.

Terry and Haydn Hasty, Kathleen Edelman, and Vicki McCoy for the inside then out approach.

Tony Ruccione, Frank Edmondson, Nick Bazin, Rob Werstler, Joe Morris, Bobby Sabas, Garry Mitchell, and Bob Lawson for being the childhood and college friends I did not deserve.

Thank you to the parent-coaches I learned from: Tim Bailey, Misti Bailey, Steve Crowe, Mark Kalb, Kevin Ross, Denise Moss, Tim Stanfill, Jon Meder, Tad Goss, Rick Bonniwell, Kevin Ellington, Jason Williams, Gordon Weaver, and Keith Costo.

The 2030 group of the early 2000s—Lyne Askins, Emery Hoyle, Ryan Noel, Mike Johnson, David Lucas, and Mindy Gautreaux—the forward thinkers who love the land *and* people.

My future bosses who mentored me: Megan Reed, Nick Byrd, Stacy Armitage, Dave Gonzales, Laurel Barnhill, Chris Cooley, Daffny Pitchford, Chris Swanson, Rebekah Martin, John Tirpak, Catherine Phillips, Shaun Sanchez, Christine Ogura, Ernie Clarke, Durwin Carter, Holly Gaboriault, Linh Phu, Will Meeks, Carolyn Swed, and Steve Reagan. Thank you for stepping out and stepping up.

Kim McClurg and Troy Littrell, for passion and conviction.

Keaston White and Kennan Adams for perseverance.

Janet Ertel, Steve Seibert, and Beth Goldstein for kindness and professionalism.

Stephanie Bruner, Brett Hunter, Vince Carver, and Betty Jarous for selfless service.

Kathy Burchett, Vic Coffman, Jane Whaley, Anitra Firmenich, Chuck Hunter and Jon Wallace for pursuit of excellence.

Thank you to the Regional Directorate Team, the ladies who kept them straight, the NWRS...

Thank you to my life examples:

Patricia Viker, my mother, for optimism and humor.

Arne Viker, my father, for patience and helpfulness.

Ellen Viker, my stepmom, for advice and common sense.

Erik Viker and Brenda Fabian for intellect and adventure.

Paul and Gretchen George and Amy Dixon and Dusty Dixon for faith and family focus.

Cotton George and Anne George for enjoying the simple things.

Madelyn Edwards and Gene Edwards for savoring the finer things.

Karen Reccia, Billy and Michelle Nicholson, Sue and John Durdaller, Tracy and Charlies Durdaller, Lisa and Matt Pizzo, and Janet and Mike Savastio for love of family and enthusiasm for life.

Ryan Noel, Chris Swanson, Brett Hunter, and Keith Weaver, for calm wisdom and collaboration.

Jenny Sears and Al Stubblefield for generosity.

Ricky Ingram and EJ Williams for mentoring and taking a chance.

Mark Musaus, the brother-uncle-father-friend-mentor-Ranger Buddy amalgamation that could change the world if more met their "Mark."

Emme Viker, daughter, for listening and insight.

Taylor Viker, daughter, for kindness and joy.

Matthew Viker, for curiosity and creativity.

Dane Viker, for loyalty and strength of character and conviction.

Mary Viker, the only love of my one life, for being the best example of humility and selflessness...and for being the one who can hold me accountable.

Citations

1. *Cambridge Free English Dictionary*, Cambridge University Press, 2016, www.dictionary.cambridge.org.

2. *Mere Christianity*, by C.S. Lewis, 1952. HarperCollins Publishers, 195 Broadway, New York, NY, 10007. www.harpercollins.com

3. *Leader Slips*, by Tony Sutherland, 2019. Tony Sutherland Ministries, Inc. 508 Westwind Way, Ball Ground, GA, 30107. www.tonysutherland.com.

4. *He Bear She Bear*, by Stan and Jan Berenstain, 1974. Random House, Inc., New York. NY.

5. *Citing strained force, Air Force cuts dozens of extra duties,* by Jared Surbu, 2016. Federal News Radio. www.federalnewsradio.com.

6. *Don't Waste Your Life*, by John Piper, 2009. Crossway, 1300 Crescent Street, Wheaton, Illinois, 60187.

7. *How to Be a Good Boss in a Bad Economy*, by Robert I. Sutton, 2009. Harvard Business Review. www.hbr.harvardbusiness.org.

8. *A Sand County Almanac*, by Aldo Leopold, 1949. 198 Madison Avenue, Oxford University Press, Inc. New York, NY, 10016.

9. *Good to Great* by Jim Collins, 2001. HarperCollins Publishers, Inc., 10 East 53rd Street, New York, NY, 10022.

10. *The 4 Disciplines of Execution*, by Chris McChesney, Sean Covey, and Jim Huling, 2012. Simon and Schuster, 1230 Avenue of the Americas, New York, NY, 10020.

11. *First, Break All the Rules*, by Marcus Buckingham and Curt Coffman, 1999. Simon and Schuster, 1230 Avenue of the Americas, New York, NY, 10020.

12. *Building a Story Brand*, by Donald Miller, 2017. HarperCollins Leadership, 195 Broadway, New York, NY, 10007.

13. *10 Simple Strategies to Improve Performance Conversations and Change Trajectory*, co Dan Rockwell, 2016. "Leadership Freak" blog, www.leadershipfreak.wordpress.com.

14. *Simplification Made Simple*, by Wally Bock, 2016. "Three Star Leadership" blog, www.threestarleadership.com.

15. *Rethinking Trust*, by Roderick M. Kramer, Harvard Business Review, 2009. www.hbr.harvardbusiness.org.

16. *What's Needed Next: A Culture of Candor*, by James O'Toole and Warren Bennis, 2009. Harvard Business Review, www.hbr.harvardbusiness.org.

17. *Team of Teams*, by General Stanley McChrystal, 2015. Penguin Random House LLC, 375 Hudson Street, New York New York 10014.

18. *Social Intelligence and the Biology of Leadership*, by Daniel Goleman and Richard Boyatzis, 2009. Harvard Business Review, www.hbr.harvardbusiness.org.

19. *Accelerate: Building Strategic Agility for a Faster-Moving World*, by John P. Kotter, 2014. Harvard Business Review Press, 60 Harvard Way, Boston, MA, 02163.

20. *Helping*, by Edgar H. Schein, 2011. Berrett-Koehler Publishers, Inc., 1333 Broadway, Suite 1000, Oakland, CA, 94612-1921.

21. *The 7 Habits of Highly Effective People*, by Stephen R. Covey, 1989. Simon & Schuster, Inc., 1230 Avenue of the Americas, New York, NY, 10020.

22. *The Practice of Adaptive Leadership*, by Ronald Heifetz, Alexander Grashow, and Marty Linsky, 2009. Harvard Business School Publishing, 60 Harvard Way, Boston, MA, 02163.

23. *How Well Do You Know the Story of You*, by Eric J. McNulty, 2016. "S+B Blogs," www.strategy-business.com

24. *The Carrot Principle*, by Adrian Gostick and Chester Elton, 2009. Free Press. A Division of Simon & Schuster, Inc., 1230 Avenue of the Americas, New York, NY, 10020.

25. *How to Politely Disagree, According to Science*, by Michelle Kinder, 2017. Time.com.

26. *Dad's Playbook – Wisdom for Fathers from the Greatest Coaches of All Time*, by Tom Limbert, 2012. Chronicle Books, LLC, 680 Second Street, San Francisco, CA, 94107.

27. *10 Principles of Strategy through Execution*, by Ivan de Souza, Richard Kauffeld, and David van Oss, 2017. Strategy+Business magazine, Issue 86, Spring 2017.

28. *The 7 Tools of Great Leaders*, by Art Petty, 2017. www.govexec.com/excellence.

29. *The Principle of the Path*, by Andy Stanley, 2008. Thomas Nelson Inc., 501 Nelson Place, Nashville, TN, 37214.

30. *Scrum: The Art of Doing Twice the Work in Half the Time*, by Jeff Sutherland and J.J. Sutherland, 2014. Crown Business, www.crownpublishing.com.

31. *The Problem with Saying 'My Door Is Always Open'*, by Megan Reitz and John Higgins, 2017. Harvard Business Review. www.hbr.harvardbusiness.org.

32. *Switch*, by Chip Heath and Dan Heath, 2010. Broadway Books, Crown Publishing Group, Random House, Inc,. 1745 Broadway Street, New York, NY, 10019. www.crownpublishing.com.

33. *The Paradox of Choice*, by Barry Schwartz, 2004. Harper Perennial, 195 Broadway, New York, NY, 10007.

34. *Immunity to Change*, by Robert Kegan and Lisa Laskow Lahey, 2009. Harvard Business Press.

35. *What Leaders Really Do*, by John P. Kotter, 1990. Harvard Business Review, www.hbr.harvardbusiness.org.

36. *The Heart of Change*, by John P. Kotter and Dan S. Cohen, 2002. Harvard Business School Press, 280 Soldiers Field Rd, Allston, MA 02134.

37. *Visioneering*, by Andy Stanley, 1999. Multnoman Books, 12265 Oracle Boulevard, Suite 200, Colorado Springs, CO 80921.

38. *Hand Me Another Brick*, by Charles R. Swindoll, 2006. W Publishing Group, P.O. Box 141000, Nashville, TN 37214.

39. *Everyone Communicates Few Connect*, by John C. Maxwell, 2010. Thomas Nelson, Inc., 501 Nelson Place, Nashville, TN, 37214.

40. *Sense of Urgency*, by John P. Kotter, 2008. Harvard Business Press. Boston, MA.

41. *The Richest Man Who Ever Lived*, by Steven K. Scott, 2006. Waterbrook Press, 12265 Oracle Boulevard, Suite 200, Colorado Springs, CO 80921.

42. *7 Men*, by Eric Metaxas, 2013. Thomas Nelson, Inc., 501 Nelson Place, Nashville, TN, 37214.

43. *To Get People to Change, Make Change Easy*, by Tania Luna and Jordan Coehn, 2017. Harvard Business Review, www.hbr.harvardbusiness.org.

44. *The Next Level: What Insider Know About Executive Success*, by Scott Eblin, 2011. Nicholas Brealey Publishing, 20 Park Plaza, Suite 115A, Boston, MA, 02116.

45. *The Speed of Trust*, by Steven M. R. Covey, 2006. Free Press, A Division of Simon & Schuster, Inc., 1230 Avenue of the Americas, New York, NY, 10020.

46. *The 21 Irrefutable Laws of Leadership*, by John C. Maxwell, 1998. Thomas Nelson, Inc., 501 Nelson Place, Nashville, TN, 37214.

47. *The 3rd Alternative*, by Stephen R. Covey, 2011. Free Press, A Division of Simon & Schuster, Inc. 1230 Avenue of the Americas, New York, NY, 10020.

48. *What's So Amazing About Grace?*, by Philip Yancey, 1997. Zondervan, Grand Rapids, MI, 49530. www.zondervan.com

49. *Principle-Centered Leadership*, by Stephen R. Covey, 1990. Simon & Schuster, Inc., 1230 Avenue of the Americas, New York, NY, 10020.

50. *The 360 Degree Leader*, by John C. Maxwell, 2005. Thomas Nelson, Inc., 501 Nelson Place, Nashville, TN, 37214.

51. *Nudge: improving decisions about health, wealth, and happiness*, by Richard H. Thaler and Cass R. Sunstein, 2008. Yale University Press, 302 Temple St, New Haven, CT, 06511.

52. *An Enemy Called Average*, by John L. Mason, 1993. Honor Books, PO Box 55388, Tulsa, OK, 74155.

53. *The Work of Leaders*, by Julie Straw, Mark Scullard, Susie Kukkonen, and Barry Davis, 2013. Wiley, One Montgomery Street, Suite 1200, San Francisco, CA, 94104.

54. *5 Gears: How to Be Present and Productive When There Is Never Enough Time,* by Jereme Kubicek and Steve Cockram, 2015. John Wiley & Sons, Inc., 111 River St, Hoboken, NJ, 07030.

55. *Leading Change*, by John P. Kotter, 1996. Harvard Business School Press, 280 Soldiers Field Rd, Allston, MA, 02134.

56. *Managing the Unexpected*, by Karl E. Weick and Kathleen M. Sutcliffe, 2007. John Wiley & Sons, Inc., 111 River St, Hoboken, NJ 07030.

57. *The Starfish and the Spider: The Unstoppable Power of Leaderless Organizations*, by Ori Brafman and Rod A. Beckstrom, 2006. Penguin Group Inc., 375 Hudson Street, New York, NY, 10014.

58. *The Ideal Team Player*, by Patrick Lencioni, 2016. John Wiley & Sons, Inc., 111 River St, Hoboken, NJ, 07030.

59. *Man's Search for Meaning*, by Viktor E. Frankl, 1959. Beacon Press, 25 Bacon Street, Boston, MA, 02108.

60. *Pursuit of God*, by A.W. Tozer, 1948. Life Sentence Publishing, Inc., 203 E. Birch Street, Abbotsford, WI, 54405.

61. *Rethink Happiness*, by Paul George, 2018. Ave Maria Press, Inc., P.O. Box 428, Notre Dame, IN, 46556.

62. *A Christmas Carol*, by Charles Dickens, 1843. Published by Chapman and Hall, 186 Strand, London, England.

63. *How to Lead When You're Not in Charge*, by Clay Scroggins, 2017. Zondervan, 2900 Sparks Drive SE, Grand Rapids, Michigan 49546

64. *Half of us Quit our Job Because of a Bad Boss*, by Benjamin Snyder, 2015. Fortune. http//fortune.com/2015/04/02/quit-reasons/.

65. *A Light in the Attic*, by Shel Silverstein, 1981. HarperCollins Publishers, 195 Broadway, New York, NY, 10007.

66. *A Long Obedience in the Same Direction*, by Eugene H. Peterson, 2000. InterVarsity Press, P.O. Box 1400, Downers Grove, IL, 60515.

67. *Measure What Matters*, by John E. Doerr, 2018. Penguin Random House LLC, 375 Hudson Street, New York, New York 10014.

68. *Liturgy of the Ordinary*, by Tish Harrison Warren, 2016. InterVarsity Press, P.O. Box 1400, Downers Grove, IL, 60515.

69. *Uncommon Life*, by Tony Dungy, 2011. Legacy, LLC, Winter Park, Florida 32789

70. *Personal Development: Build on your strengths? Yes, and ...*, by Wall Bock. 2020. "Three Star Leadership" blog. 715 West Home Avenue, Hartsville, SC, 29550.

71. *Becoming the Totally Responsible Person*, 2019. Participant's Workbook, 3rd Edition, TRP Enterprises, Inc. 333 Summit Square Court, Winston-Salem, NC 27105.

72. *Everybody, Always,* by Bob Goff, 2018. Alive Literary Agency, 7680 Goddard Street, Suite 200, Colorado Springs, CO, 80920. www.aliveliterary.com.

73. *Ride of a Lifetime*, by Robert Iger, 2019. Penguin Random House LLC, 375 Hudson Street, New York, New York 10014.

74. *Think Again*, by Adam Grant, 2021. Penguin Random House LLC, 375 Hudson Street, New York, New York 10014.

"Leadership is hard—here's new help"